THE CHURCH AND CIVILIZATION

THE CHURCH
AND CIVILIZATION

Jerome D'Souza, S.J.

DOUBLEDAY & COMPANY, INC.

Garden City, New York

1967

Nihil obstat: Edward J. Montano, S.T.D.
                    Censor Librorum

Imprimatur: ✠ Terence J. Cooke, D.D., V.G.
                    Archdiocese of New York
                    December 1, 1966

The *nihil obstat* and *imprimatur* are official declarations that a book or pamphlet is free of doctrinal or moral error. No implication is contained therein that those who have granted the *nihil obstat* and *imprimatur* agree with the contents, opinions, or statements expressed.

1384935

CONTENTS

PREFACE

This is not a "learned" book in the sense of its being a cold and dispassionate statement of facts and of logical conclusions drawn from them. The title of the book might lead the reader to think that it is an authoritative exposition of the stand taken by the Church in the face of the cultures that develop independently of her spiritual inspiration. But in reality it is a very personal work, though this may not appear on the surface. It is an attempt to present as objectively as I could, but with deep conviction, certain historical facts and the ideas that have grown and evolved in my mind around these facts in the course of many years. They are answers to questions which I was compelled to ask myself in the situations in which I was placed. I must explain this even at the risk of appearing egoistic.

Born and brought up in India in a family converted to Catholicism many generations ago by Portuguese missionaries,[1] I have always experienced the deepest satisfaction in the faith and the practice of it. Even when the practice was not particularly fervent, I kept up continuous reading of books of Catholic doctrine and history, and tried to understand them more and more deeply. But I belonged to a family and "com-

[1] They were accustomed to give Portuguese names to their converts. That explains the diffusion of these names among many Catholics of Indian race.

munity" a good deal westernized in its ways and outlook, and in the books I read the faith was expounded by Western writers who took for granted the universal validity of their culture. Moreover, that early impressionable period coincided with the years before World War I when the prestige of European culture in educated circles in India was still immense. However, the non-Christian youth around me—in school and college—were being captured by the ideas of the Indian renaissance, the cultural and political reawakening of India. Mahatma Gandhi's achievements in South Africa were coming to be known though he had himself not yet returned to India. But the Catholic youth of my country generally stood aloof from the national movement because of its involvement with a Hindu religious revival.

But we could not long ignore the call to take part wholeheartedly in the national effort to revive the energies of our people, to undertake the political and social reconstruction of our country. How could we resist the magic of Mahatmaji's words and ideas? Men in my situation were torn between two loyalties—to the spirit and culture of Catholicism as we understood it then, and to India pleading that all her sons should stand together in the cause of national betterment. This led to study and reflection, and to the first steps in the process of understanding the relation between religion and culture.

Subsequent events gave me other occasions to pursue the line of thought started then. My university studies in Madras and a year's teaching in St. Joseph's College, Trichinopoly, brought me into the Tamil country.[2] I entered the Society of

[2] The States of the Indian Federation are "linguistic," that is, based on differences of language. Tamil, the oldest of the Dravidian languages, is spoken in the Madras State which includes the Madurai and Trichinopoly districts where De Nobili began his experiment. By origin, I belong to the Kannada-speaking Mysore State

Jesus in the Madura Mission, where De Nobili had begun his great movement of "adaptation." I came into contact with Catholics whose cultural affinities and outlook were wholly Indian. It was a new experience, and opened up horizons till then unsuspected.

My knowledge of Western culture in earlier years was through the literature and history of England. Later on, as a Jesuit, I made my theological studies in France and Belgium. This gave me knowledge of types of European culture strikingly different from the spirit and outlook of English culture. I realized that the "Western civilization" of which Indian publicists spoke was a far more complex phenomenon than they or I suspected.

Thereafter the years of active ministry brought me a closer knowledge of the thought and spirit of India—Hindu and Muslim—enabling me to discover, as it were, my own country in middle life. That period culminated in membership in the Constituent Assembly of India in 1946. Later on I was appointed several times as one of the delegates of India to the United Nations General Assembly, and made fairly extensive lecturing tours in the States and Canada. That was my initiation into another facet of Western civilization noticeably different from the European. And everywhere—in South India, in England and France and Belgium, in the United States and in Canada—the Church was at home and had its part in the cultural evolution of those countries. All this supplied me with matter pertinent to my problem and helped me to understand better the role of the Church in the growth of national cultures.

During these recent years I have lived in Rome, at the Headquarters of the Society of Jesus and under the shadow of St.

---

though my own mother tongue is Konkani, a language closely allied to Marathi, both Indo-Aryan languages.

Peter's and the Vatican. My work involved fairly wide travelling in Europe, Asia, and Africa. I have watched currents of life and culture from every quarter of the world cross and recross unceasingly around me. Finally came the crowning experience—the vision of the Ecumenical Church in the years of the Council.

This book attempts to present the image of the Church as it emerged in my mind in the light of all these experiences. That is why I said that it is not a "learned" but a personal book. At this time and from this place I cannot even give chapter and verse for many of the quotations interspersed in it. The reader will have to take them on trust. But I think I can vouch for the substantial accuracy of whatever I have adduced as fact in these chapters.

I have committed myself to writing the thoughts contained herein in the hope that they may be useful to others who may be facing problems similar to mine; that they, too, may succeed in integrating their varied experiences in their understanding of the mystery of the Church, and thus attain to serenity of mind on this issue of the Church and secular cultures. I should be doubly happy if any of them should take up one or other of the aspects touched on in this essay and produce a really learned work on it.

J. D'SOUZA, S.J.

Rome
13th May 1966
Feast of St. Robert Bellarmine

INTRODUCTION

THE MYSTERY HIDDEN IN GOD

The Christian believer as he looks at the world is perplexed and scandalized by what he sees. It is hard to discern the presence of God and the operation of a loving Providence in this confused movement of men, often acting aimlessly and, more often, violently in opposition among themselves. Nature herself, in which it is easier to see "army on army of inalterable law,"[1] is, in other ways, "red in tooth and claw with rapine," and seems thus to give to man the example of violence and self-destructive hatreds. Cardinal Newman summed up this vision of a world "without God and without hope" in a famous passage; it seemed to him that either there is no Creator or "the human race is implicated in some terrible original calamity. It is out of joint with the purposes of its Creator." So he concluded that "thus the doctrine of what is theologically called original sin becomes to me almost as certain as that the world exists and as the existence of God."[2]

There is but one way to understand and interpret this scene of pain and confusion, one key that opens out the orderly recesses behind this surface of contradictions: to see them all in relation with Christ, his Incarnation, his atonement, his abiding presence in the world through his Church. This is "the mystery hidden in God from all eternity," that he would re-

[1] Meredith's sonnet "Lucifer in Starlight."
[2] *Apologia,* Part VII.

make all things in Christ, and restore to man in even richer measure than was granted to him in his primitive state the privileges which he had destined to this younger creature of his: *"mirabiliter condidisti et mirabilius reformasti."*[3]

Although in the strict sense redemption and elevation of man to sonship through Christ Our Lord is a totally gratuitous gift of God, it is not easy to believe that the God of infinite goodness would have decreed the creation of a world where sinful man was destined to remain forever in his misery. In the fulness of time this creature of earth, this amalgam of spirit and matter, was to rise to a dignity which the angels themselves were not granted. For in saying "Thou art my son, this day I have begotten thee," to his only begotten son, God spoke it to all those who were to be united to him by their common humanity, and were to be made more intimately one with him in the mystical body of the total Christ.

We speak of "the mystery of Christ"; and he who says "mystery" says something that, in the last analysis, is beyond human comprehension. This, however, does not imply that it is beyond an ever-deepening understanding of its multiple facets. So with the mystery of Jesus. To his Jewish contemporaries, the mystery consisted mainly in the assertion that the God of Sinai was speaking to them in the person of the son of Joseph, whose mother was Mary. But when the Resurrection confirmed the faith of the disciples in Christ's divinity, and when the Holy Spirit, given to the Church on the day of Pentecost, began to open the minds of the Christians to the hidden aspects of that mystery, they began to perceive all that was implied in the tremendous fact of the Incarnation. It had made men brothers of Jesus by adoption, and it had brought into their hearts the spirit of Jesus whereby they would call God "Father." Through the sacred humanity of Jesus and the Eucharist, God

[3] Prayer before the Offertory at Mass.

had blessed and consecrated the entire world of matter itself, matter indissolubly linked with the very essence of man, his external life and his interior activity. Moreover, by the mystery of the Passion and of the Cross, God had transformed human suffering into an expression of obedience and love. Thus, out of the ruins accumulated by sin, he had laid the foundations of his New City.

The above is an application of the mystery of Jesus to the world of space, the reflection of the Incarnation in the entire universe of matter. Equally important is its extension to the world of time, the continued presence of Jesus on earth through the members of his mystical body until the final fulfilment of the kingdom by his second coming. This is "the mystery of the Church" which is, essentially, a part of the mystery of Jesus. From the very beginning Jesus had gathered disciples and apostles around him, not only to carry his message to others, but also to act in his name and to exercise powers which were properly his, such as to heal the sick and to drive out evil spirits. These powers he confirmed and completed in the time between his Resurrection and his Ascension. He gave them a participation in his own eternal priesthood, he gave them power to preach and interpret the word of God, to baptize, to forgive sins, to offer the Eucharistic sacrifice. From the beginning, too, he preached the brotherhood of all men, more specially of those who "hear the word of God and do it": they make one family, they are his "mother and brothers and sisters." He told them that the simplest act of charity, done to the least of his brethren, was done to him. He exhorted them to be one, united among themselves, and to be, with him and through him, united to God.

Over this family—apostles, priests, and people—Christ constituted Peter as head, giving him power to bind and to loose. "Thou art Peter, and it is on this rock that I will build my church; and the gates of hell shall not prevail against it. And

I will give to thee the keys of the kingdom of heaven; and whatever thou shalt bind on earth shall be bound in heaven and whatever thou shalt loose on earth shall be loosed in heaven" (Matthew 16:18–19).

If the nature and prerogatives of the Church constitute a mystery and are part of the mystery of Jesus, as we have said, it is obvious that an adequate presentation of it is beyond human capacity. It belongs to that order of truths whose intimate meaning should grow upon one in prayer and meditation, and by the operation of the Holy Spirit enter somehow into the texture of our daily life. But it is not too difficult to describe its lineaments, based on ideas and expressions which are to be found in Scripture. At the same time, it is necessary to remember that the understanding which we have of these things today has been the result of a long process of thought and maturation. Such "gradualness" too enters into the plans of God for redeemed humanity.

Scripture speaks of "the people of God," of "the kingdom of God," of the "Temple of God," of the "Mystical body of Christ," of the "Spouse of Christ." It speaks of an external and hierarchical structure—of apostles and disciples and people; it describes the powers of the ministry being communicated by the "laying on of hands." It also speaks of the internal activity of the Holy Spirit within the soul, imparting to it the virtues of faith, hope, and charity; of the inner growth and transformation of each "until Christ is formed in them," and that to such a degree that they "live, no longer they but Christ lives in them."

This recapitulation of the names and of the activities by which the nature of the Church is indicated in scriptural sources reveals, as we said, both an external and visible society and an internal and spiritual activity. In the course of the centuries, when the nature of the Church had to be defined with particular reference to the problems and controversies that were repeatedly emerging, first one and then another of those aspects was emphasized. The Protestants of the sixteenth century for the most part denied the necessity for a hierarchical Church, and conceived the Church as a purely spiritual, invisible body whose members were known only to God, the author of their predestination. This led, on the Catholic side, to an overemphasis of the external and juridical aspect. Such exaggerations, in theory and in practice, have led to serious misunderstandings of the nature of the Church. They have obscured some of the richest and deepest elements of the mystery of Jesus. The modern movement, devotional and theological, towards a better understanding of the Church as the mystical body of Christ, enables us to hold in hand all the threads and to arrive at a balanced and comprehensive description of it. Its most luminous expression is to be found in the great Conciliar decree *Lumen gentium,* and the encyclical of Pope Paul VI *Ecclesiam suam.*

For the purposes of this chapter, we may synopsize that teaching in the following way. The Church is the body of all those whom God has called to be united to his son Jesus by faith and love. That body was founded by Jesus himself and was given a hierarchical structure with Peter at its head and the apostles under him. The visible organization of the Church and the sacerdotal ministry handed over to the apostles and to their successors has for, its ultimate end, the birth, conservation, and growth of the life of grace within the soul. This grace, which is a participation in the divine nature, unites them to Jesus and, through him, to the Trinity. It makes them brothers of Jesus and sons of God. Together, they constitute the mystical body of Jesus which, with its divine head, makes up "the total Christ."

Christ died for all; and it is the will of God that all men should be saved—that is, be brought into union with Jesus, to sonship of God, and to the heritage of the beatific vision. Of this salvation the Church is the instrument, and it is her task to bring all men into her fold by preaching the Gospel to them and moving them to faith and the acceptance of the Sacraments. It is within this context that we may understand what is meant by saying that outside this Church there is no salvation. There are many good men who do not know the Church as she is, and who do not recognize her as the unique instrument of salvation; yet they may have dispositions equivalent to an implicit readiness to enter the Church if they had sufficient knowledge of her. In this way they may receive the grace of Christ. The accepted expression to describe their state was to say that they belong to the "soul of the Church."[4] Thus, the Church in her totality is not necessarily conterminous with her visible boundaries.

Though the doctrine of the Church in all its fulness, like most other dogmas, has been "developed"—that is, understood and expressed better and better—in the course of the centuries under the guidance of the ever present Holy Spirit, it is not the creation of theological speculation. Theological reflection has built on the unshakeable foundations of Scripture, on the teaching and actions of the apostles. We saw that the Church

[4] Theologians no longer like to use this expression "soul of the Church" because in a real sense the Holy Spirit is the soul of the Church, and because the distinction between a visible and an invisible Church would not be quite correct. There is but one Church, which is visible. Non-Christians who are in a state of grace belong to it invisibly. Hence some theologians have called such men "anonymous Christians." This doctrine of the salvation of those who do not belong visibly to the Church was exposed by Pius IX in the encyclical *Quanto conficiamur* 1863. See also the letter of the Holy Office on the case of Rev. Leonard Feeney to Cardinal Cushing (1949). The most authoritative exposition of the doctrine is to be found in the Vatican II's *Declaration on Non-Christian Religions,* and in the *Decree on the Missions,* and most important of all, *Lumen gentium,* No. 16.

was founded in its essential lineaments by Jesus himself during his public life and after his Resurrection. One of his last actions was to breathe on the apostles and give them power to forgive sins, and to command them to preach to all creatures to the very ends of the earth. But it was Pentecost which marked, in a decisive way, the birth of the Church. Even as the historical Jesus was conceived by the Holy Spirit in the womb of the Blessed Virgin, so the mystical Jesus was born by the pouring of the Holy Spirit on those who had adhered to Jesus by faith and love.

More than all others, it was St. Paul who understood—from the very first vision of Jesus on the road to Damascus, and from his words: "Saul, Saul, why persecutest thou Me?"—the nature of the Church as the mystical body, nourished and sustained by the Eucharistic banquet. St. John emphasized the inner life of the Church, the intimate union of all Christians with Christ because of the grace of Christ which flows through all of them as the sap runs from the vine into the branches. He also brings out with incomparable clarity the role of the Eucharist in maintaining the life of grace and union with Jesus. The struggle of the Church against the powers of darkness is always present before his eyes. He sees the Church not as the final kingdom of God, but as the preparation for the final triumph and the confusion of the enemy by the second coming of Christ. The Gospel of St. John, the Acts, the Apocalypse, and the Epistles of St. Paul contain all the basic elements of the doctrine of the Church as the kingdom of God, as the spouse and mystical body of Christ.

Let us now examine briefly the Church today and see whether we discern in it the stamp that is on Jesus, whether she constitutes the abiding presence on earth of Jesus himself.

Jesus was the teacher of the hidden mysteries of God. The only begotten son "who is in the bosom of the Father" came down to teach us these mysteries. He taught as no man taught; he taught not as the scribes and pharisees, but as one having authority. The Church, too, is a teacher; she is *magistra*. She speaks to mankind on the things that pertain to their last end with an authority and an assurance that astonish men of the world who are lost in their doubts and contradictions and "blown about by every wind of doctrine." They may disagree with her; they may oppose her teaching; but they cannot ignore her, or fail to hear and note what she says. Her "voice goes out to the ends of the world." She speaks not only clearly but emphatically, with that resonance of language which has been her heritage from the Epistles of St. Peter and St. Paul to the decrees of the Vatican Council.

Jesus fed the hungry, healed the sick, and comforted the afflicted. What nation or association of men practices the "corporal works of mercy" with the heroic devotion of the Church, of her ministers and religious orders? Christian men and women have sacrificed themselves in their hundreds and thousands in order to succour the poor and the suffering—the prisoner, the orphan, the aged, and the incurable. They have put aside the fairest promises of life to consecrate themselves to obscure and laborious lives in order to bring the brightness and warmth of Christian love to the lonely and the abandoned. Undoubtedly the modern welfare state does much for the disinherited of the world—but its inspiration has come from the example of the Church. Even today, there are many who would willingly give up the abundant but impersonal charity of the state in favour of the love and human sympathy of the disciples of Christ.[5]

[5] In India, for instance, the national government strives to right the wrongs of centuries and gives to the so-called "untouchable" and the aborigine many forms of gratuitous assistance which is not given to the same extent to the converts to Christianity. Nevertheless hundreds of them turn to the Christian missions precisely by

Our Lord proved the authenticity of his mission by his power over the demons and by the miracles which he worked. He pleaded with his adversaries, telling them that, if they did not believe his words, they could believe at least the works he did. Have such signs ever ceased in the history of the Church? Rather, has not the word of Jesus been often verified, that greater things than what he himself did his disciples would do? The canonizations of the saints and the history of many famous sanctuaries contain unquestionable proof of miraculous interventions and are an indirect confirmation of the claims of the Church.[6] As in the time of Our Lord, these signs do not convert to the faith all those who see them or see the evidence of them. But they leave even the unbeliever baffled by what he admits to be their inexplicable nature.

Our Lord was the Prince of Peace. Unwearied is the effort of the Church to rise above national rivalries, to preach the gospel of universal brotherhood, to denounce racialism and every form of the oppression of the weak by the strong, and thus to diminish the causes of war and international strife.

Jesus was the Holy One of God, the God-Man of utter purity and uninterrupted prayer. We say that the Church is holy. She is holy not only in her essence by the grace of the Holy Spirit who is her "soul," but by the testimony of resplendent holiness which has never been wanting in her, no, not even in the dark days when her visible rulers fell into a scandalous worldliness. All her saints—martyrs, doctors, confessors, and virgins —have this in common: they have borne the "stigmata" of the Lord Jesus, and have been recognized by all as his faithful imitators, as "other Christs." They have also been, and always, men

---

reason of this human contact and sympathy, and, of course, by attraction to the person of Christ, the Man of Sorrows.

[6] I would mention in particular the history of the apparitions of Lourdes and the constantly recurring miracles, carefully verified and registered by the Bureau des Constatations.

of prayer as Jesus was a man of prayer. From the churches and monasteries and convents of the Church, from every faithful Christian household there has risen to God the unceasing murmur of prayer, of praise and adoration and thanksgiving and humble supplication for pardon and grace. "On your walls, O Jerusalem, I have placed my watchmen. All day and night they sing the praises of my name."[7]

Our Lord "suffered under Pontius Pilate, was crucified, died and was buried, and on the third day rose again." So says the Creed, which we have all repeated from childhood. Do we realize how true this is of the Church? From the Good Friday of Calvary to this day the Church has been crucified in one or another part of the world; some member of her body has been bruised and bleeding in testimony of the Passion of the Lord. From the time of Herod, who martyred James the "brother of the Lord," to the prisons and concentration camps of the "tolerant" twentieth century, there has been no epoch when the entire Church was at peace. Again and again has been brought against her the accusation made against Jesus: "He calls himself a king and prevents people from paying tribute to Caesar." There have been moments when she seemed dead indeed, and her exultant enemies thought they had sealed the tomb and suppressed the "scandal" forever. But like Jesus, again and again the Church has risen from the tomb: from the catacombs, from the anarchy of the barbarian invasions, from the havoc of the Great Schism, from the Protestant Reformation, from the deluge of the French Revolution. These were "resurrections" on the universal plane. But there have been similar miracles of survival on a smaller scale in many countries,—"second springs," Newman called them—in England, in Holland, in many parts of Germany, in Japan and other mis-

[7] A "response" in the Roman Breviary.

sion territories. No human institution has known such a survival.

Lastly, in the Mass, Christ has left us a memorial of the Passion, of the immolation of himself on the Cross in obedience of the Father, and also of his Resurrection. Thus, his unique sacrifice is renewed every day and every moment in the Church, "from the rising of the day to the setting thereof." In the Eucharist, the mystery of the Church appears in all its depth; its stupendous and incomprehensible reality brings home to us the union of all men in and through Christ by faith and love.

It is true that in the long and chequered history of the Church, in its human and visible manifestations, some of these lineaments of the face of Christ have been obscured, and in the eyes of many they still stand obscured. Nothing more harmful and damaging to the designs of God for the salvation of men can be imagined than to mistake the true nature of the Church, to say, as so many say, that Christ and his Church are two entirely different entities, one lovable and adorable, the other human, ambitious, sinful, tyrannical—that they would willingly accept Christ but not the Church.

Perhaps even in the defects which led to tragic misconceptions of her true nature, the Church in a mysterious way shared the infirmities of which the suffering Christ, loaded with the sins of the world, bore the marks on his divine countenance. Today, however, many clouds have been dispersed, many stains washed away. Something of the beauty of her face stands revealed now before the world. More easily men recognize in her the beginning of that celestial Jerusalem, that "blessed vision of peace" towards which she is leading her children. The deliberations of the Vatican Council, more than any factor, have been responsible for that recognition. In those solemn assizes the world saw the Church reflecting on herself and on her true nature, declaring what she is and wishes to be

among the children of men. Pope Paul VI, taking as his point
of departure the decrees and declarations of the Council, is
revealing himself as a veritable "doctor of the mystery of the
Church." Once Jesus, speaking to Philip, said, "Philip, who
sees me, sees the Father." Today the Church can dare to say,
"Who sees me, sees Jesus."

CHAPTER I

CHRIST: HEART AND CENTRE OF THE HUMAN STORY

If the eternal plan of God in decreeing the creation of the world was to restore or "recapitulate" all things in Christ and to make him the crown of the world of nature and man, it follows that human history has a divine significance, and that Christ is the heart and centre of the human story. All the strands of material growth and evolution, all the currents of human life and activity, were to lead to *him* and converge in *him*, under the rule of an all-wise and all-knowing Providence. After his appearance and life on earth, all the activity of regenerated man must proceed from him and must subserve his design of perfecting the people of God for his second coming and for the establishing of his everlasting rule. The Incarnation was in this way to touch and transform all human reality.

But the human family cannot be separated from the material environment in which man is placed. The greatest achievement of modern science has been to reveal to us the intimate connection between all material things and to demonstrate how even the free and soaring spirit of man is inextricably involved in the world of matter and in the action of its forces. This is true not only of our own planet, lost in the vastness of space, but of the entire universe, whose movements and evolution have their part not only in producing the specific conditions in which man lives on earth but also in giving "form and pressure" to every minute and every action of his life. Long before scientists demonstrated this truth, poets, with their intuitive vision, had perceived it. Francis Thompson had the mystic insight that enabled him to see how "all things to one another linkéd are; you cannot touch a flower without troubling of a star"; and Tennyson, going even further and grappling with the very nature of being, said to his "Flower in the crannied wall," "Little flower, if I could but know what you are, I would know what God and man are."

We may, therefore, with every scientific justification and spiritual assurance, contemplate the process of material creation, from the very first appearance of dispersed matter in space, as having been directed in the plans of God to the emergence of man, and, in the fulness of time, to the coming of the son of man.

In the light of Christian doctrine, that orientation towards man and the God-Man should be considered from two angles. Insofar as creation is the bringing into existence of "participated being," of "secondary causes," it should be seen in relation to the mystery of the blessed Trinity, to the generation of the Word of God in whom all things were created. Vatican Council I defined that man, from the knowledge of visible things and by the exercise of his natural reason, can ascertain the existence of a creator. But the idea of creation itself, the why and the how of the existence of participated and dependent being which is nevertheless free and responsible, presents formidable metaphysical problems. Only the revelation of the hidden and inaccessible life of God in the Trinity, unsuspected by unaided human intelligence, indicates the possibility of a solution satisfying to the inquiring mind.

But the relation of the Word of God to creation comes home to us in quite another way and with more compelling force when we see him as the head of a new creation, the leader of a new humanity, the lord of a world of man and nature made new by the Incarnation. The little handful of matter which went to make the body of Jesus, the little morsel of bread

which is changed by his power into his own body and blood,
touch and transform the entire universe and make it incan-
descent with the reflection of the Divinity. To such an ultimate
end was the evolution of the earth and the preparation of a
home for man directed by the Creator; the earth with all its
riches was to be harnessed to the service of man, ultimately of
one man.

Our concern, however, in this essay is not the study of the
Incarnation in its relation to the entire universe of nature and
man, but to one particular facet of human activity which has
assumed special importance at this time. How do the presence
and spirit of Christ, as they come in contact with new races
and peoples in the course of the uninterrupted expansion of
the Church, affect the civilizations which those races and peoples have built up? Those civilizations have been a response
to the conditions of time and place in which these people
lived their personal and social lives. They have varied and
multiplied for many reasons—the geographical peculiarities of
their physical homes, the racial characteristics of those who
built them up, the skills and traditions which they brought
with them as they broke off, perhaps, from a larger human
unit in order to find a new home. Above all, these civilizations
bear the impress of the free thought and action of men—
leaders, thinkers, poets, and artists—whose emergence cannot
be explained as the result of predetermined forces. They influenced their fellow men and gave a direction to the social
evolution of their people by the exercise of personal freedom
under the Providence of God. It is therefore clear that each of
the many civilizations of men has been formed and allowed to
develop, not independently of God's decree to "restore all
things in Christ," but within the framework of his plan for all
mankind.

A study of the relations of the Church to civilizations is particularly urgent at the present time because the entire world

is being opened up to the message of the Gospel with a facility of communications and interchange of ideas on a scale never known before. The world thus laid open to the message of Jesus—or better still, in view of what we know to be the essence of that message, to adhesion to the person of Jesus and assimilation into his mystical body—is one which contains, as I said, many and diverse civilizations. The children of those civilizations are proud of their cultural heritage and of the hold it has on their minds and hearts. Under the pressure of modern nationalism, and in reaction against foreign cultures, almost all the old non-Christian cultures are undergoing a process of reform and reaffirmation. For reasons which we shall see later on, they tend to look upon Christianity, not only as the bearer of a religious and spiritual message, but as the sponsor and secret ally of those foreign cultures which they seek to resist. The salvific will of God (which in concrete language means the progress of the Church and the extension of the mystical body) thus encounters a human obstacle of peculiar gravity.

Today, when men speak of civilization, having no clear-cut definition of it in their minds, they think mainly of a certain advanced state of the arts of social living. Their ideas about it tend to be confused with what, in our day, we are accustomed to call the "standard of life": the degree of convenience and comfort achieved in the domestic and social arts; in lodging, food, and clothing; in literature and the fine arts; in government and political organization. The exaggerated importance given to the material side of life in the modern popular concept of civilization is due mainly to the tremendous technical progress of our times and the unparalleled degree of material prosperity to which Western civilization has attained.

In reality, however, it is not possible to give a satisfactory idea of what "civilization" is without including in it a moral as well as an intellectual element. The intellectual aspect will be easily understood. The fine arts and the social arts, whose

progress is an essential criterion of civilization, cannot flourish
without an intellectual expression of the principles which un-
derlie them. The arts and the social sciences, together with
speculation about these principles, constitute a culture and are
the higher aspect of civilization. Equally, the arts of social living and the pursuit of the common good, which is the basic
obligation of organized society, imply an over-all view of man's
nature and destiny and a clear concept of moral good—in other
words the beginnings at least of a philosophy and religion. And
this, in turn, establishes a certain hierarchy of values in deter-
mining the duties of man as a member of society. Among the
peoples of Asia particularly, religion—Hinduism, Buddhism,
Shintoism, Confucianism, Islam—has inspired great and noble
civilizations. In some cases, religion has put a stamp on the
men of those societies which has determined the spirit and
quality of their domestic and social arts and now affects even
the simplest actions of their daily life.

It is a common criticism both within the Church and outside,
more particularly among the followers of non-Christian religions in mission countries, that the Church has been identified unduly, and according to some irrevocably, with what is
known as Western, or more plainly European, culture. So faithful and perceptive a son of the Church as Hilaire Belloc said
squarely that the "Faith is Europe, and Europe is the Faith."
The missionary methods followed in certain areas seemed to
imply that the Church herself, in the person of her authoritative messengers, accepted that dictum. If that is really so, we
must either deny the universality of the Christian message or
assert that God is not the author of the diversity of races and
civilizations; that the human race is destined not only to unity
of endeavour towards a common spiritual goal but to the dull
uniformity of a standardized culture. Either proposition is, on
the face of it, untenable.

No one, however, would pretend that the Church has always

had, from her very beginnings, a clear-cut idea of what her attitude should be towards the diverse civilizations she was to encounter on her onward march. We cannot deny that errors have been committed, that in the process of groping towards right solutions the bright countenance of Jesus in the mystical body has been obscured before the eyes of many; and that in consequence precious occasions of extending the kingdom have been lost.

Those who have true insight into the "mystery of the Church" will not be surprised at this. Jesus is God incarnate. He has taken upon himself human nature with all its weaknesses, its miseries and infirmities. But the "Incarnation" of the mystical Jesus in the human family implies a human element in the Church, and differently from Jesus, a human element including errors and sins on the part of individuals. Those who contemplate the "miracle of the Church"—her faithful testimony to Jesus, her manifestation of his life in herself such as I have described, her triumph over obstacles, and her survival not "as a remnant of herself but full of strength and youthful vigour," as Lord Macaulay proclaimed—those who contemplate and take pride in this miracle must also pause to consider and understand the "scandal" of the Church, the human weaknesses among her rulers and children. They might even learn to draw comfort and spiritual strength from it. As in the case of individuals, for whom personal sins and all the sorrow and humiliation which they bring may be the means of entering more fully into the mystery of the sacred Passion and humiliations of Christ, so for the Church. The errors and sins in which she never acquiesces, against which in shame and anger she ever struggles, urging her children to do penance in sackcloth and ashes, may also be a mysterious participation in the objection of the "Man of Sorrows, knowing infirmity," who was "made sin" for our sakes.

That is the first consideration to be kept in mind in viewing the tactical blunders and errors of policy which rulers of the Church have committed in their attitude towards human civilizations. The second and equally pertinent consideration is the role of time in enabling the Church to understand all the implications of the deposit of faith she has received from Jesus and the apostles. The principle of slow growth and development seems to mark all the manifestation of the designs of God in the universe of matter and space. The spirit of man is dazed and bewildered by the perspectives of endless time and space, which the evolution of the material world reveals. But far from shaking our faith in God, they should confirm it and should fill us with awe as being a reflection of his very infinity.

The growth of life from the first living cell to the emergence of *homo sapiens* took millions and millions of years. Fallen man struggled with the forces of nature without and the passions within for thousands of years, all the while clinging to the hope of the promised redeemer. How long it took for that hope to be fulfilled, from the first faint announcements in the earliest Scriptures through the ever-clearer prophecies of the Psalmist, of Isaias, of Daniel, till at last the precursor could point out to the living Lamb of God who was to take away the sins of the world! Jesus, himself; how cautiously did he not unveil the secret of the true nature of his messianity, lest a fanatical and worldly minded generation should take umbrage at the doctrine of his eternal generation and his atonement in sorrow and pain.

Today the scholars and theologians of the Church, in the light of twenty centuries of Christian history, understand better the principle of the "development of Christian doctrine," which Newman first enunciated in a book replete with personal drama and spiritual passion. The clash of doctrine and of religious ideas, whatever their origin—errors from within, or penetration of alien concepts from without—led the Church, through her councils and the pronouncements of the popes, to interpret and clarify and define whatever was implicit in the sources of revelation. Thus, the great dogmas regarding the Incarnation and the two natures of Christ, the place of Our Lady in the Christian economy, the nature of the Sacraments, the authority of the Church and of the pope, have been defined in the course of ages and are expressed in "creeds," which Catholics accept unquestioningly and firmly believe to be truths revealed by Jesus.

Nonetheless, the attitude of the Church to the civilizations she encounters, and with which she has to come to terms in some way in order to establish herself in their midst, is not the subject matter of a precisely defined dogma. It is, rather, a question of method, of the practical handling of emergent situations in the light, certainly, of unquestionable dogmas; it is a question of policy which involves declarations of principles by the ordinary *magisterium* or teaching authority of the Church. Such occasions call for reflection by the Church about her own nature and about her role in the world.

In the course of her long history the Church has had repeatedly to make such reflection, to "enter into herself," to analyze her past actions and decisions, to study anew the exigencies of the mission entrusted to her in order to determine her role in the ever-widening horizons which have opened out before her. In Vatican Council II and in the declarations of Pope Paul VI we have the latest, and in some ways the most significant, of those efforts at self-scrutiny—to know herself, to read the signs of the times, and to decide effectively the attitude she must adopt in the world of today. But this is not the first time the Church has been seriously concerned about her attitude towards the secular and cultural activity of the men around her. As she came out of the limitations of the first Judaeo-Christian community of Jerusalem, and then out of the catacombs, and spread out in ever-widening circles around her, she has had occasions, some more decisive than others, to define that attitude.

For the purpose of the present study, we shall consider briefly four changes of environment and four periods of reflection that led the Church to define her stand in the diversity of cultures which successively confronted her. The first occasion was when the Church of Jerusalem, linked with Israel and bound up with Jewish practices, went out to the Gentiles and converted the Greek and Roman world to Christianity. The Church Christianized the composite Greco-Roman culture of the Mediterranean basin. Already at that stage she was beginning to assimilate that diversity of civilizations, of external modes of living and forms of expression, which was essential for her if she was to be truly catholic, i.e., universal. The next great occasion was the conversion of the barbarian and Slavonic nations and the subsequent slow emergence of national cultures. She Christianized them, too, and at the same time enriched herself in the cultural sphere by a process of give and take. Next came the explosions of the sixteenth century, the return to the classical past, and the opening of new worlds in Asia, Africa, and America. A fresh period of reflection was inevitable, a new process of give and take, a new synthesis by which Christian culture was enriched again by new strands from East and West. It was an age of unrivalled missionary expansion, and the period of those far-reaching efforts at "adaptation" which will enable us to understand the true spirit of the Church and her basic attitude to such civilizations as are inspired and fostered by non-Christian religions. Finally we come to the present day, when the so-called Christian culture of Europe has been secularized to such an extent that we speak of the "post-Christian era" in the West. The Church must define her attitude to this new world around her and also to the revived national cultures of ancient peoples who have thrown off the political yoke of Europe. In these successive expansions, as we shall see, there was no "identification of the Church with Western culture"—indeed there has never been one single Western culture with which to identify herself. Rather, we shall see her as the mother and teacher of *all* people,—*mater et magistra*. We shall see that, in these successive "epiphanies" of Jesus and of his mystical body, Christ through his Church has received homage and "royal gifts" from East and from West, and from every race and nation on earth.

CHAPTER II

THE CHURCH IN THE
GRECO-ROMAN WORLD

The process of reflection by the Church about her nature and role in the world began, as I said, very early. The environment in which she had her birth and first developments was already a complex one. The people of Israel, among whom she had her origin, looked upon themselves as the chosen people of God, segregated from the rest of sinful and idolatrous humanity in order to preserve and proclaim the worship of the one "true and living God." But, even in this restricted and rigidly controlled group, diversities had already crept in and created dissensions. There had been, about two centuries before Our Lord, the forcible attempt of the Greek kings of Syria—in particular Antiochus IV—to impose pagan customs on the Jews and to wrest them away from their allegiance to the Law. Though this was defeated by the Machabees and fidelity to the prescriptions of the Law had become the rule among the Hebrew people, the penetration of Hellenic ways in civil and social life had not ceased. The love of Greek culture—language, dress, and social manners—had created a class of Hellenized Jews, looked upon with contempt and dislike by the pharisaic group which had carried to fantastic lengths the observance of ritualistic prescriptions regarding food, dress, and sabbath observance. There were also groups of "God-fearing men" from among the Gentiles who had become proselytes to Judaism and were in some way aggregated to the chosen people.

The Christian Church, born in Jerusalem among the stricter

observers of the Law, had soon to define its attitude to these different groups. The "elders" had first to make up their minds about the converts from among the Hellenized Jews. Since the Christians in the Church of Jerusalem were still part of the Jewish community and attended the synagogues and fulfilled all the prescriptions of the Law, the Hellenized Jews were not at first given the consideration which they claimed and merited in the light of the new teaching. Their faith in Jesus and the virtue of the baptism they had received entitled them to full equality with the Judaeo-Christians. The Church of Jerusalem therefore established the order of deacons to look after them in a special manner. Stephen, the protomartyr, began his heroic life of charity by ministering to them. It was this which drew the attention of the orthodox Jews to the danger of permitting the Christian ferment to work in the synagogue, and they stirred up the persecution which ended in the martyrdom of Stephen.

The conversion of the Hellenized Jews went on rapidly, and the Deacon Philip was most assiduous in this ministry. He also began the conversion of the Samaritans, whom the non-Christian Jews regarded as heretics. The Christian community at Antioch was, in large part, made up of Hellenized Jews. Barnabas became their accredited apostle, and was destined later to be the right-hand man of St. Paul and to take a leading part in opening up a far wider horizon before the nascent Church.

After the problem of the Hellenized Jews, there was that of the attitude to be adopted towards the proselytes who were uncircumcised. The Gospel had already given a remarkable example of the faith and charity of one such, the Centurion of Capharnaum, whose immortal words, "Lord I am not worthy that you should come under my roof," ring across the world every day in the Mass. But the crucial case was that of Cornelius, narrated in Chapter X of Acts, who was baptized with-

out circumcision and received into the fellowship of the
Church. Earlier there had been another striking incident of this
kind when Philip instructed and baptized the Eunuch of
Candace, Queen of Ethiopia, after interpreting for him the
deepest of the messianic prophecies of Isaias (Acts 8:27–39).
It is a memorable scene, only a little less dramatic than the
one on the way to Emmaus when the unrecognized Master
explained to the two disciples, "beginning from Moses, the
things that were concerning him." 1384935

The decisive step in the proclamation of the universalism
of the Christian message against the sectarianism of the Jews
was to come later with St. Paul. Was the redemption of Jesus
universal? Was the Gospel to be preached to the Gentiles,
that is, to the pagan nations in the full sense of the term, the
men who lived in idolatry and in ignorance of the God of
Israel? Was the departure he was advocating wholly new and
revolutionary, or was there a foundation for it in the Scriptures?

It is often said with reference to evolution in the material
order that all processes of growth and development start with
an entity which contains in an embryonic form, or which at
least foreshadows, the complexities which it will ultimately attain. This has its applicability to the world of thought. Any
basic idea destined to energize and ramify in the world of
thought and of action, by a process of genuine development
and not merely by mechanical accretion, must possess from
the first the germ of those future developments. It was so with
God's plan of universal redemption. The need to prepare a
suitable environment for the proclamation of the Gospel had
led to the practical segregation of the Jewish people and their
stern social exclusiveness. Only thus was it possible to preserve
them from the idolatries and the "abominations" of the heathen
world around them. The fact that their leaders rejected the
Messiah does not make the preparation any the less necessary

since it assured the reception and understanding of the Gospel message by the first disciples and apostles of the Lord, who were all from Israel. The ultimate vocation of the Gentiles, however, had been foreshadowed in Scripture from the very outset.

In the Old Testament the clearest prophecies concerning the vocation of the Gentiles to salvation and to inclusion in the kingdom of the Messiah are to be found in the Psalms: "Thou art my Son, this day have I begotten thee: ask thy will of me and thou shalt have the nations for thy patrimony" (Ps. 2:7); then in even stronger language in Isaias: "Here is my servant. My spirit rests upon him, and he will proclaim right order among the Gentiles. . . . I have summoned thee, taking thee by the hand, and protecting thee . . . to shed through thee light over the Gentiles" (Isaias 2:1 ff.). Simeon was to take up this last word in the Temple with the child Jesus in his arms: "This is the light which shall give revelation to the Gentiles" (Luke 2:32). Equally significant is the place given in the Old Testament to holy Job, who was not an Israelite but an inhabitant of the "land of Hus." In the New Testament the universally recognized symbol of the vocation of the Gentiles was the adoration of the Magi, related by St. Matthew, who was a true Israelite fully imbued with the Jewish tradition. Nevertheless he describes how outside Israel the grace of God had prepared the hearts of these just men to seek and adore the new-born Saviour.

Our Lord himself said that he had come for the lost children of the house of Israel, "because salvation is of the Jews" (John 4:22). But he did not exclude the Gentiles in his ministry. He marvelled at the faith of the Syrophoenician woman and of the Centurion of Capharnaum. He revealed his sublimest doctrine to the Samaritan woman at the well of Jacob and told her that the time had come when true adorers were to adore God neither on the Garizim nor in Jerusalem, but that God was a spirit and was to be adored in spirit and in truth (John 4:23). In other words, the true adorers were all men of good will on earth.

But the full and open application of this universalism was to begin only after the refusal of Israel to listen to the message. Saul of Tarsus—Israelite-born, Hellenic in culture, citizen of Rome—was the man destined for this great mission.

The inner command from the Holy Spirit which Paul and Barnabas had received was confirmed by the signs and miracles which were worked among the converted Gentiles. The Judaeo-Christians were alarmed at this development. Paul, however, asked that the apostles and the leaders of the Church of Jerusalem should meet together, hear them, and then decide the question once for all. Thus in the year 49 was held the first Council of the Church, the Council of Jerusalem, so astonishingly similar to the later councils of the Church in the practical problems which called for it, the freedom of discussion, the final decision by Peter, and the general acceptance of that decision as part of the authoritative teaching of the Church. Paul and Barnabas related the wonders that had taken place among the converted Gentiles who had not been circumcised and had not accepted the prescriptions of the Jewish Law. Peter rose and declared that this yoke, which their fathers themselves had found it impossible to carry, should not be imposed on the Gentiles. James, the most respected of the elders of Jerusalem and a faithful observer of the Law, accepted the decision: provided the Gentiles abstained from sinful pagan customs, they were not to be disturbed (cf. Acts 15). It was a momentous decision. The bark of Peter was to leave the sheltered waters of its Palestinian home and launch out on the wide ocean.

Everyone knows the story of that early Christian expansion in the Roman world, associated forever with the incessant journeys of St. Paul; its vicissitudes, its triumphs, and its failures are reflected in the Epistles. The "mystery of Jesus" and the doctrine of the mystical body are exposed therein with the fire and force of one who, quite apart from divine inspiration, must be pronounced one of the greatest masters of the spoken and the written word. In pursuance of our theme of the Church as teacher of men, and indirectly as the maker and moulder of civilizations, let us now look at the religious and cultural setting into which St. Paul carried the message of God's plan "to restore all things in Christ."

In the Roman Empire, in which Christianity first established itself, there reigned the widest diversity of races and cultures. All the branches of the Aryan race were represented there, most of the western Aryans—Greeks, Latins, Celts, Germans, and Slavs—and almost certainly in the eastern provinces of the Empire some representatives of the Indo-Iranian branch that had settled in Persia and India. Then there were the Hebrews and Arabs and other peoples of the Semitic race, the populations of North Africa, and the huge number of slaves from many parts of the world. Speaking their various languages and bearing the stamp of their diverse civilizations, they jostled and mingled in the forums of Rome and the other cities of the empire.

The predominant culture was that known as Greco-Roman: the thought and the arts of Greece, the law, the polity, and the military science of Rome. But there was an extraordinary intellectual and religious ferment in this Greco-Roman world. The prevailing pagan polytheism on which the divinity of the emperor and the cult of the state were based did not preclude the activity of many philosophical schools—for example, Sophists, Epicureans, Stoics, Platonists. Above all, there was a new vogue for Oriental religions, esoteric cults, mysteries Greek and Persian, which were being disseminated with great rapidity among the upper and middle classes. These cults were not without some redeeming features that created a climate favourable to the diffusion of Christianity. There were vague aspirations towards the coming of some great prophet who might bring wisdom and salvation to all men.[1] Virgil himself, in the *Fourth Eclogue,* seems to have expressed this general aspiration—so much so that for centuries Christendom included him among the prophets of Our Lord. There was a consciousness of the corruption of the flesh and of the need for asceticism or of magic ceremonies to overcome it and to liberate the soul for union with the Divinity. Along with this, there was also a wild and degrading immorality practiced in the name of religion.

The Roman world, then, was astonishingly modern in its mingling of currents from all parts of the world, from Asia, Africa, western and northern Europe. It was an epitome of the many worlds of thought and external forms of civilization which the Church was to meet in the course of her future history.

Père de Grandmaison, in his *Jesus Christ,* describes the *milieu evangélique* in which Jesus preached the Gospel as stirred by many new ideas, intellectual and spiritual, and compares it, among other places and times, to "the India of Tagore and Gandhi." I think this is even more true of the Roman world in which the apostles and the Apostolic Fathers preached Christianity. There was a cultural and religious ferment similar to the one which Asia experiences today from the impact of the West on her ancient civilizations. It was in such a Greco-Roman world that the thinkers and pastors of the

[1] Such beliefs were common in India and Persia, and the Eastern cults brought them to Rome. In India in particular the idea of the appearance of God in human form, *Avataras,* was familiar to all. Alexander's conquest of a part of India had established cultural contacts between ancient India and Europe.

Church were first schooled. They learned there, at that early stage of Christian history, the art of dealing with ideas and cultures which had originated outside Christianity. They helped to establish a "Roman tradition" which has since rarely failed to guide the Church in similar situations.

The superficial similarities of the ideas and ceremonies of some of these religions of the Roman world to the teaching and the Sacraments of the Church have led "liberal" and sceptical critics to develop theories of Christianity as a human construction growing out of the conditions of its birth and diffusion, as the result of skilful borrowing by well-intentioned or astute men. It is not necessary to enter into this question, which is outside our purview. The spirit and instincts of man are the same everywhere. If his inner aspirations led him to express himself religiously in gestures and ceremonies which resemble those of Christianity, it only argues that God chose to express the content of his authentic revelation in terms and symbols intelligible to all. There will be "borrowings" all along the way in the course of the history of the Church: languages, forms of art, external gestures of worship, which Christianity will adopt, transform by her inner spirit, and "baptize" in Christ. It is this principle of the assimilation of external forms without losing consciousness of her own identity that enables the Church to enter into and transform human activity. She thus draws out the implications of the mystery of the Incarnation in all the spheres of the created universe. It is in this sense that she is the mistress and maker of civilization and not the slave of any single system of human culture.

There were, however, two elements which the Church could not compromise or permit to be tampered with: the first was the nucleus of revealed truths, the deposit she had received from the Lord and from the apostles; the second was the immediate conclusions in the practical or ethical sphere which these theological truths implied, or the principles which they presupposed. The creation, man, compound of spirit and body, the spiritual destiny of man, the Fall, the atonement and restoration of man's dignity through Christ, the Sacraments as means of grace, the authority of Peter and of the teaching Church—these constituted in more senses than one the "rock" on which her immense structure was to be built. If these were safe, then the Church was ready to accept and to bless the outer garments of every civilization. From the beginning she accepted the fact of diversity within her fold and gloried in it. Obviously that outer garment, before she Christianized it and made it her own, had often covered a body and a soul different from hers. In other words, the language and the art forms of a given civilization may have expressed or recalled a mythology and a concept of man's nature and destiny alien to her own teaching, but in the Church's use of them they acquired a new meaning.[2] It is in this sense that the Church remakes civilizations. But she does more. She enriches them in the secular field with social concepts and principles of universal validity which flow from her theological doctrine. Thus in carrying out her mission to "restore all things in Christ" until the world is ready for his second coming, she transforms and enriches the heart and spirit of non-Christian civilizations. "The Church," Cardinal Newman observed in *The Development of Dogma* (Ch. VIII), "has been ever sitting in the midst of the doctors both 'hearing and asking them questions'; claiming to herself what they said rightly, correcting their errors, supplying their defects, completing their beginnings, expanding their

---

[2] The best example I can give of this are many Sanscrit religious terms now used by Catholics in India without suspecting that among Hindus they have a different connotation: *moksha* (heaven), *naraka* (hell), *prasada* (grace), *prayaschitta* (penance), *dhyana* (prayer).

surmises, and thus gradually by means of them enlarging the range and defining the sense of her teaching."

By this process the Church Christianized the many civilizations and religious systems of the Roman Empire, taking something from each one and giving to all her inner spirit. From the Greeks she took precision of concept and clarity of language for the definition of her doctrine; from the Romans she took the ideas of law and social government and the organization of her hierarchy. From the East she took the ideal of eremitical and monastic life and many external forms of worship and liturgy. And to all of them she left intact their heritage in language and art, dress and manners, all "the external garment of cvilizations" of which I have spoken. This process, however, was not an easy and straightforward one. It included inevitably much experimenting and learning by mistakes—not mistakes in the sense of errors of doctrine, but "blunders in action" as Tertullian said so well of St. Peter's indulgence to the Judaeo-Christians in spite of his better judgement.

Inevitably, too, this process involved conflicts not only with the old paganism but also with heretical sects within the Church, sects influenced in their aberrations by the doctrines of the schools and cults around them. Newman speaks (*Ibid.*) of conflict

with the Oriental Mysteries, flitting wildly to and fro like spectres; with the Gnostics who made knowledge all in all, despised the many and called Catholics mere children in the Truth; with the Neo-Platonists, men of literature, pedants, visionaries or courtiers, with the Manichees who professed to seek truth by reason not by Faith; with the fluctuating school of Antioch, the time serving Eusebians and the reckless versatile Arians; with the fanatic Montanists and the harsh Novatians who shrank from the

Catholic doctrine without power to propagate their own. These sects had no stay or consistency, yet they contained elements of truth amid their error; and had Christianity been as they, it might have resolved into them; but it had that hold of the truth which gave its teaching a gravity, a consistency, a sternness and a force to which its rivals, for the most part, were strangers.

In the enumeration above, Newman writes of the heresies and controversies which afflicted the Church in the earlier epochs; most of them affected the Greek Church. Two later heresies, however,—those of the Donatists and of the Pelagians —recall the figure of the greatest thinker of that era in the Western Church, St. Augustine. He, more than all others, illustrates the role of the Christian writers who were in the process of adapting and Christianizing the cultures of the Roman Empire: first the Apostolic Fathers, with St. Ignatius of Antioch and St. Ireneus; then the Apologists, with St. Justin at their head; then the Fathers of the Church in its three branches; the lesser known Syrian or Oriental Fathers, of whom the best known is St. Ephrem; the great Greek Fathers, Origen, Athanasius, Basil, the two Gregories, John Chrysostom; the giants of the Latin Church, Ambrose, Jerome, and Augustine. It was these men—masters of the language and of the thought of the ancient world—who baptized the pagan culture of their time and transmitted it to posterity in a Christian garb. St. Augustine exercised an unrivalled influence on the thought and religious life of the Western Church for eight hundred years. *The City of God* and the *Confessions* have exercised a unique influence on Christian thinking and the evolution of Christian cultures.

From this rapid survey one fact emerges clear and incontrovertible: in the Catholic Church there was, from the beginning, a great diversity of cultures and modes of thought. The Church adapted herself to all of them and in turn adapted their riches, philosophical and artistic, to her own needs. In the Catholicism which emerged from the catacombs and became the religion of the Roman Empire, there were at least three recognizable cultural currents—the Oriental, the Greek, and the Latin—each with its own linguistic and artistic traditions, and all of them authentically Catholic.

CHAPTER III

THE EMERGENCE OF EUROPE AND
OF NATIONAL CULTURES

The Roman Empire, built up by the military and political genius of a great people, seemed to be a structure made to last forever, so firmly were the parts welded together to form a whole, so surely were the most distant provinces linked to the centre by personal and juridical ties. The cultural divergences between the eastern and western sections of the empire were reconciled by the concept of common citizenship, by the rule of law, and by a broadly uniform administrative system. The conversion of this empire to Christianity brought a new element of unity while it did away with the all-embracing and semidivine power of the pagan emperor.

The Christians were devoted citizens and firm believers in both the durability and the providential nature of this imperial organization. When the empire eventually collapsed under a series of successive blows, the Christians were utterly bewildered and looked upon the disruption of it, not only as the end of a stable political order, but of the Christian order itself. We know that it was not so; that the Church, though she received cruel wounds in the course of the process, emerged as the dominant influence in the European order, which succeeded the Roman order. From the triumphant Roman Church of Theodosius and St. Ambrose, to the European Church of Innocent III and the Thomistic Synthesis, eight centuries were to pass (the sixth to the thirteenth). It is outside my purpose to chronicle the political events of this historical change, but its main features may be briefly indicated, in a geographical rather than a chronological order.

The division of the empire into its eastern and western halves had sown the seeds of a rivalry which was to prove fatal in many ways. Barbarians gradually infiltrated the Western Empire by way of the army and through important administrative posts. While the west was being battered at its frontiers by other and more savage barbarians, the Eastern Empire, proud of its Greek culture and often at battle with the Roman Church on points of doctrine, failed to come to its rescue. The outlying provinces of the west were lost one after another, in fact if not in theory, and barbarian kingdoms were being set up there. In the fifth century, the successors of the western emperors had no effective jurisdiction beyond Italy. Unable to defend Rome against the barbarians, they had shifted their capital to Ravenna. From 410 to 560, Rome was repeatedly sacked by Goths, Huns, and Vandals. General Belisarius finally reconquered the city for Justinian, the eastern emperor, and for nearly two hundred years Italy was a province of the Eastern Empire. Greek Exarchs ruled in Ravenna. The glory of ancient Rome had ended in tragedy and ruin. That of Papal Rome had yet to begin.

The prosperity of the Eastern Empire, which reached its zenith under Justinian in the sixth century, was not destined to last indefinitely. The religious autocracy of the emperors, that seed of Cesaropapism which Constantine himself had introduced in his patronage of the Church, led to continual interference in doctrinal matters by the emperors. They took sides in the unending controversies about Nestorianism, Monophysism, and Monothelism; later, they gave impetus to the controversy of Iconoclasm. They also encouraged the claims of Constantinople to equality of rank with Rome. At first, under this imperial influence, primarily political motives led to frequent dissidence between the popes and the patriarchs of Constantinople. It was Photius who gave a theological turn, late in the ninth century, to the disagreements by the famous *filioque* controversy.[1] Photius himself died in communion with Rome, but under Michael Cerularius, in the eleventh century, the breach became permanent, and the two churches exchanged excommunications which were to stand until 1966 when, as a symbol of hope for Christian unity, they were withdrawn by the pope and the patriarch of Constantinople.

In the meantime the new power of Islam was establishing itself with irresistible force in Arabia and the nearby countries, and was wresting from the Eastern Empire some of its fairest provinces. The faith of the people had been already weakened by their having to accept and then give up now one, now another, of the successive heresies we have mentioned. Bishops were exiled or recalled according to whether the emperors rejected or accepted the Orthodox faith. The Arabs, triumphant everywhere, became masters of the Mediterranean, established themselves in Spain, and overran southern France. At last they were stopped at Constantinople by Emperor Leo III in 717, and at Poitiers by Charles Martel in 732. After this, Western Christendom organized itself against the Muslims, stopped their advance, slowly reconquered Spain and Moorish France, and through the Crusades carried the war into the enemies' camps.

These religious expeditions might have been a golden opportunity for the reunion of the Eastern and Western Churches. The behaviour of the Western crusaders, however, produced exactly the contrary effect. The conquest and sacking of Constantinople in 1204 and the setting up of a Latin emperor there confirmed the passionate antipathy of the Greeks towards the Latins and made every future effort at reunion fruitless or, at

[1] The Greeks denied that the Holy Spirit proceeded from "the son also" (*filioque*).

best, a political expedient. It is only in our own day, after the meeting of two holy and humble men Paul and Athenagoras, that we can look forward to the healing of a breach for which there is no serious religious justification.

But though the Eastern Church was lost, materially, to the unity of Catholic Christendom, it had made its contribution to the formation of Christian thought and art. The Oriental and Greek Fathers had left writings which were to be a permanent part of the Catholic heritage. Early Christian art was profoundly influenced by Byzantine models, and during the years of Byzantine dominance in Italy the Greek artists filled the churches of Rome and of Ravenna and other cities with the loveliest examples of Byzantine architecture and mosaics of breath-taking beauty. There are still twenty million Catholics of the Oriental Rite who enrich the liturgy and spirituality of the Church by their contributions, and, under God's Providence, they may be the means of restoring union between the Catholic and Orthodox churches.

The western provinces of the Roman Empire were in the meantime undergoing a radical transformation, and in this the Church was playing a decisive role. Many of the new semi-independent barbarian kingdoms of the West were founded and ruled by leaders who had entered the service of the empire and had become Christians. Some of them became Arians when the emperors supported that heresy, and the Catholic Church in their territories was subjected to cruel persecution. But with the conversion from paganism of Clovis, the King of the Franks, in 498, the tide turned in favour of the Catholics. One after another the Arian ruling houses became Catholic. New territories were evangelized. St. Patrick evangelized Ireland in the fifth century and set up a church that was destined thereafter to play a great role in the Church. St. Boniface converted a great part of Germany and the as yet unconverted Germanic people of Central Europe in the eighth century. The conversion of the Scandinavian nations was completed in the twelfth century.

About the same time, the Slavonic nations, too, beginning with Poland, accepted the Gospel. Here there was some trouble owing to the rivalry between the Eastern and the Western Church. Russia seems to have been converted by missionaries from Constantinople after the breach made by Photius, though there is some evidence of an earlier Catholic penetration there. The Slavs of the Eastern Rite adhered to Constantinople for the greater part, but others—the Poles, the Czechs, the Slovenes, the Croats, the Lithuanians, the Bohemians—were Catholic and have remained so.

The conversion of the Western nations and their adhesion to the papacy coincided with the growing indifference of the Eastern Empire to the safety and dignity of the papacy when its independence was threatened by some of the still pagan and untamed Germanic rulers. From this menace the papacy was liberated by Charlemagne, the grandson of Charles Martel. Charlemagne had been anointed and crowned emperor by Pope Leo III in 800, and ruled a new Roman Empire, an immense grouping of nations between the Elbe and the Pyrenees, and west to east, between the North Sea and Bohemia. He was not only a faithful son and protector of the Church but a great ruler. He enforced justice in those rough times and among his turbulent people, and promoted the arts of peace. He fostered letters, organized schools, with the help of such great scholars as Alcuin and Eginhard, and thus ensured the transmission of the most precious elements of Roman civilization to the newly converted nations. But before we describe how this was done, we shall make a brief survey of the external fortunes of the empire and the papacy till the thirteenth century.

Charlemagne's protection of the Church contained those same elements of Cesaropapism which Constantine had bequeathed to the Eastern Empire. In some ways the situation was even more perilous for the Church of the West because the culture and authority of the bishops made them desirable as civil officers of the empire. Thus a large number of them became princes and barons and owed, in that capacity, allegiance—the "fealty" of a feudal vassal—to the king or emperor in addition to their obedience to the pope. Thus, both under Charlemagne and his successors, the bishops came to be dominated by secular rulers. This led eventually to the appointment of men as bishops who had no spiritual qualification whatever and, in the course of time, to the development of the most shameful partisanship and promotion of family fortunes. Charlemagne's empire collapsed under his weak successors, but the ecclesiastical abuses continued with even greater effrontery in the smaller kingdoms into which it dissolved.

The great difference between the Eastern and the Western Church was that, notwithstanding the weakness of many popes and their many unhappy surrenders to secular authority, the Western Church kept up a continuous struggle for its independence. That famous struggle between the empire and the papacy contains some dramatic events. The best known is the clash between Hildebrand (Gregory VII) and Emperor Henry IV, which ended in the submission of the emperor at Canossa in 1077. Then followed the long struggle against Frederic Barbarossa on the same question of the investiture of bishops, and after him with Frederick II. The victory of the papacy was complete under the masterful Innocent III. Not only was the independence of the papacy and of the Church proclaimed and established, but the superiority of the spiritual power over the temporal, of the pope over the emperor, was also affirmed and accepted. And this was true not merely in the sense of the primacy of the spiritual over the temporal, but in the practical exercise of direct authority over the emperor by the pope. The pope was henceforth to choose or to confirm the choice of the emperor, and to communicate to him as from God his power to rule the Christian people. The bishops and abbots were to be elected by the clergy, and their choice had to be confirmed by the pope. Thus, the Church became a vast supranational "empire" whose spiritual authority and temporal power were accepted by the entire Catholic people. To rule this immense grouping of nations and churches an elaborate legal and fiscal system was developed and a centralized bureaucracy, the Roman Curia, was created. Its officials had to be trained to the complex work of government. The canonist and the diplomat thus entered into the governing machinery of the Church.

We must now turn to our special theme of the Church as *magistra*, as teacher not only of theological truth but as guide and moulder of human culture in all those aspects in which civilization and culture have affinities with the basic Christian concepts of man's nature and destiny. For not only theological doctrines, but even the forms and spirit of Church government have a cultural resonance. We have seen that the Church had Christianized and given a deeper significance and wider diffusion to some of the most characteristic features of Greco-Roman civilization. It is these aspects that the Church transmitted to the new nations, giving to them an intellectual climate in which their national cultures were to develop. They would certainly develop, each in its own way; they would retain their own languages, evolve external forms and conventions of social living, domestic arts, and particular types of artistic expression in keeping with their own genius. And thus it is that the culture, we might even say the civilization, of every European country is different from that of another. Such differences between the European countries, between Spain and France and Italy, Ireland and England, Germany and Poland and the Slavonic nations, is so obvious that it is un-

necessary to labour the point. These divergences extend to
the religious sphere also, to architecture, painting, music, and
types of devotion and religious sentiment. But their soul is
Christian and Catholic in an unmistakable way because the
basic ideals—the concept of the scope and significance of human life, the objectives and method of intellectual training, the
structure of ecclesiastical and political government—were
everywhere the same. It is precisely these common elements
which manifest the continuity between the Greco-Roman
world and the agglomeration of European nations.

Let us note here that this "corpus" of elements of civilization
of universal value was to be enlarged and enriched by the
Church in the course of her sojourn among different nations.
With every widening of the horizon she was, and continues to
be, in a position to contribute a larger body of basic principles
to a subsequent and resulting synthesis. Obviously this process will go on until humanity evolves a world civilization consistent with national diversities; but, for the present, our concern is with the civilizing role of the Church in the Europe of
the new nations. Let us see how and to what extent she did
this.

The Church exercised a civilizing influence primarily
through instruction, both religious and secular. The Church of
the new nations was a rural Church made up of people who
had settled in the country and whose communities were unlike those forming the main part of the Church in the Roman
Empire. To these rough and unlettered masses who knew little
more than the rudiments of the faith, some kind of education
and culture had to be imparted. It was the monastic orders
which were the most effective instruments in civilizing the
rural masses. They exercised a many-sided activity. In the first
place, they were apostles and missionaries among the pagans.
The earliest and greatest missionaries were the Benedictines of
Italy, England, Ireland, and France, men who converted in

great part the new nations in succession, penetrating more and more deeply into northern and eastern Europe. Their monasteries became the centres of instruction in reading and writing, and in the development of agriculture; gradually, they also became the promoters of refined forms of art—music, painting, and architecture. They were the heralds and preachers of moral reform in times of unparalleled brutality and immorality.

As bishops, churchmen were instrumental in organizing the government of the Church and, often, also that of the state. It was through them that the Roman concepts of political organization and civil government were handed over, with due adaptation, to modern Europe, and through modern Europe have become part of the principles of civil government throughout the world.

The great monastic foundations of Cluny, Citeaux, and Premontré, with their rapid diffusion throughout Europe, played a role in civilizing the people of Europe which it is difficult to exaggerate. The Cistercians and the Premonstratensians in particular established systems of instruction for their priests in philosophy and theology which may be described as the first seminaries of the Catholic Church. This was to be further perfected by the Dominican order, which came later, and whose vocation was more decidedly intellectual. These monastic schools led in the thirteenth century to the founding of the universities, among them Paris, the greatest of all the cultural centres of Europe. After the monastic orders came the mendicant orders, chief among them being the Franciscans and the Dominicans. They were teachers and moral guides among the rank and file of the Christian people, who were always subject to the abuses resulting from political disorder, or who were tempted to revert to pagan excesses under the influence of wealth and power. These preachers carried to the people in their own language the culture and learning which were until then the privilege of those who attended schools and universities or lived in monastic surroundings. They helped to form the modern languages of Europe.[2] Their popularity was extraordinary; in the course of a few decades they had spread over the whole of western Europe, with hundreds of houses and thousands of members.

While the Franciscans and Dominicans were primarily preachers and reformers of morals, they were also active in the universities. Their three great Doctors, St. Albert the Great, St. Bonaventure, and St. Thomas Aquinas, perfected the medieval Scholastic synthesis in which was reached perhaps the highest point of Catholic intellectual achievement.

We must glance at some of the features of that Thomistic synthesis because in it we can discern the beginnings of what we can only call Christian humanism in a broad sense of the term. It was to develop in many directions in the course of the centuries and is still in the process of being completed and perfected. It is this humanism which forms the core of those cultural principles of universal value which the Church as teacher communicates to the civilizations she encounters. The foundation of the Thomistic synthesis is the philosophy of Aristotle, which the Arabs transmitted to the West and which the Muslim conquest of the East and of a part of Europe brought to the knowledge of Christendom. In the forms in which Aristotelianism was presented by Averroes and Avicenna, two great Muslim teachers, there was real danger of

[2] It would be difficult to exaggerate the role of Christian preaching, of doctrinal and spiritual instruction, and of the lives of saints, in enriching the vocabulary and enlarging the resources of these languages in their formative period. Take the stiff diction and limited content of the earliest pre-Christian Anglo-Saxon texts and compare them with the writings of King Alfred or with the *Anglo-Saxon Chronicle*. It is like coming out of a dark forest into the broad country of meadows and streams and open skies.

a pantheistic explanation of the universe. It was the glory of St. Thomas that he freed the doctrine of Aristotle from these interpretations and harmonized it with the doctrines of the Church.

Aristotelian philosophy enabled the Scholastics to reject the "mysticism" of Platonic doctrine and to abandon the system of interpreting nature as the symbol, or allegory, of spiritual truth and the invisible world.[3] They could thus build a theory of knowledge based upon a realistic examination of the data given by the senses. By reasoning on the "universal ideas" drawn from knowledge of the external world, the Scholastics constructed the entire domain of philosophy from metaphysics to ethics, and then proceeded to show its relation to the world of faith. The reconciliation of reason and faith was their main objective, but the place given by them to sense perception as the starting point of all intellectual construction was the basis on which the European mind was to build the structure of scientific inquiry. It is significant that St. Albert the Great was a firm believer in experimentation and is considered a pioneer in the field of physics.

The concept of man's dual nature—the physical and the spiritual integrated in one indivisible person—the recognition of the objective worth of nature, man's ability to construct a valid philosophical system by reason, and his capacity to rise to supernatural dignity by faith, all constitute the heart of Christian humanism. To this must be added other elements which the struggles and experiences of the preceding centuries had made part of the Christian consciousness. The clash between the papacy and the empire had helped to establish the independence of the spiritual power and to clarify the

[3] The Scholastics rejected mysticism in a system of rational knowledge, and not as a means of suprarational illumination in the supernatural sphere.

doctrine of the two perfect societies, church and state. This distinction contained, basically, the right of the individual conscience not to be coerced in spiritual matters by the temporal power. But the full implications of this, its development into a coherent doctrine of personal liberty and religious tolerance, were to be worked out later. Herein we see the emergence of the Catholic "middle way" between theocracy and total secularism.

Equally relevant to the concept of Christian humanism was the tender devotion to the humanity of Our Lord which Franciscan spirituality promoted along with the Franciscan love of nature.[4] Already in Benedictine spirtuality the person of Our Lord, devotion to him, both in himself and as represented by one's religious superiors, had received marked attention. But the Franciscan revival carried it much further. The same trend was helped by the Dominican struggle against the Albigensian heresy and their final overcoming of the strain of Manichean dualism which it sought to bring into the Church. The cult of Our Lady and the ideals of chivalry had at the same time brought in a new concept of the dignity and role of womanhood. The foundresses of religious orders, such as St. Clare, and the great rulers of monasteries of nuns, had given to women an importance in the activity of the Church which they had never had before. Slavery was ending. The service of the poor and the redemption of captives became the object of many religious congregations. It is impossible to enumerate all the elements which made up this new attitude toward the world of nature and of man. It was a brighter vision than could have been inspired either by dualism or by pantheism.

In formulating these principles and carrying out these policies that touch at so many points the secular activity of

[4] Chesterton's *Life of St. Francis of Assisi* contains a brilliant analysis of the rise of Franciscan humanism.

man, the Church was fulfilling her role of mother and teacher in theological doctrine and also in the sphere of civilization and culture. Rarely has her achievement been so full, so varied, so harmonious as in the thirteenth century: the vision of Europe united under the spiritual power of the papacy, the philosophical and theological synthesis of the *Summa* of Aquinas, the intellectual energy displayed by the universities, the spiritual and humanitarian activity of the mendicant orders, the painting of Fra Angelico and the poetry of Dante, the architecture and sculpture of the Gothic cathedrals. It was a rare fusion of art and learning and holiness. An English poet has symbolized the union of art and philosophy in ancient Greece in a noble line: "Over Plato's homestead fell the shadow of the Parthenon." But it is even more moving to think that in the middle years of the thirteenth century, when St. Louis ruled over France, Thomas Aquinas, from the humble cell in which he prayed and wrote, might have watched the façade and towers of Notre Dame as they rose majestically in the very heart of the Ile-de-France. It was Christendom at its best and noblest.

CHAPTER IV

REVOLUTION AND RECONSTRUCTION IN THE SIXTEENTH CENTURY

The settled Christian order which had emerged in the thirteenth century after the struggles of the Dark Ages was so comprehensive and so firmly established that those who lived under it might easily have thought that it was destined to last forever. The citizens of the Roman Empire, before its disintegration, had had the same sense of security. But like the Roman, so the medieval order, too, was destined to be demolished. The Renaissance and the Reformation were to throw into turmoil all the nations of the West and to introduce an intellectual ferment in which every accepted concept and doctrine seemed open to question. At the same time, the discovery of America, and a closer knowledge of Africa and Asia, which the colonial and commercial pioneers brought to Christendom, opened up before the theologians and leaders of the Church examples of new modes of life based on old and well-established religious systems. It was necessary to study them and define their own attitude to them if they were to be gained to the faith. It was an unbelievable widening of physical boundaries and the opening of intellectual horizons around the closed world of Western Christendom. The Church, if she was to survive, had to adjust herself to them.

Of these two aspects of expansion, as we may justly call it, we shall in this chapter deal with the earlier and more fundamental, the revolution in Europe caused by the Renaissance and the Reformation. First we shall glance quickly at the seeds of dissension which lay hidden in the ideas and methods of the medieval settlement itself; then the external causes that led to the revolt against the Church and the fearful losses which she sustained; and finally her long-deferred reaction by reform and reconstruction. We shall then see a fresh example of her assimilation of new ideas insofar as they were consistent with her fundamental teaching, and her triumphant reaffirmation of her faith once again widened and enriched by the doctrinal and cultural synthesis and by the disciplinary action of the Catholic Reform.

We noted the establishment of what has been called the "superstate" of the Church in Europe, and the exercise of political power by the popes over the princes of Christendom through a highly organized curia and an elaborate system of canon law. The levying and collection of papal taxes and the heavy burdens this imposed upon many princes and their bishops stirred up dislike of the papacy and diminished its spiritual authority. At the same time the growing sense of nationalism among the different peoples of Europe made them resent this interference from one who appeared to them more and more as an Italian ruler than as the father of Christendom. So, to the dislike bred by the fiscalism of the papal administration was added increasing impatience with the endless involvement of the popes in political manoeuvres and the shifting alliances which are inseparable from the conduct of a temporal power.

The German emperors and the French kings were always busy with schemes for dominating the papacy and reducing it to dependence on their own power. This brought about at one stage the practical capture of the papacy by the French monarchy, the long exile of the popes in Avignon, and the dominance of the cardinals and popes of French nationality. This, in its turn, prepared the way for the Great Schism, which more than anything else sapped the foundations of papal authority and facilitated the success of the Reformation. A series of popes and anti-popes caused a division of loyalties in every diocese and in almost every parish of Europe. The efforts to overcome this situation fostered the development of theories of the power of the council over that of the pope, and this was actually asserted in the Council of Constance in 1414. But Constance had at least the merit of ending the Schism through the energetic action of the Emperor Sigismund. In Martin V the Church had at last a single pope to whom the whole of Christendom owed allegiance.

The restoration of unity was the signal for a serious movement of reform in the discipline of the Church and the religious observance of the people. Already very serious damage had been done to the faith of the people, not only by the scandal of the Schism, but also by certain other deeper causes. One was the decadence of scholastic learning and the influence of the Nominalist philosophy of Occam, which tended to take away all substance from the concepts through which Catholic doctrine had been enunciated. A mood of scepticism and indifference to objective truth, the spread of superstitions and practices divorced from genuine faith, were sapping the foundations of Christian life. The dreadful scourge known as the Black Death, which in the course of a few years reduced the population of some of the countries of Europe to half of what it had been,[1] carried off the most vigorous and promising section of the people, and filled the survivors, to a large extent, not with a salutary fear, but a determination to enjoy life in the world since existence had become so precarious.

Martin V initiated a strong movement of reform against corruption in high places within the Church, and against the decay of faith and morals among the masses. His successor,

[1] In all Europe it is estimated that 25 million—one fourth of the total population—were carried away.

Eugene IV, carried it forward with some energy. A number of great saints helped the Church in this earlier movement of reform: St. Bernardine of Siena and St. John Capistran; St. Catherine of Siena and St. Colette. There was also the contribution of several reformed religious congregations and brotherhoods, among whom mention must be made of the Flemish congregation of Windesheim, from which came Thomas à Kempis and that immortal classic of Christian perfection, *The Imitation of Christ*.

But this promising development was arrested by an event which is one of the landmarks in the intellectual history of Europe and indeed of the world: the revival of learning—called the New Learning, or the Renaissance. The Renaissance followed the capture of Constantinople by the Turks in 1453 and the consequent movement of Eastern scholars into western Europe. They brought with them a full and first-hand knowledge of the classics of Greece and Rome. Europe, in its mood of reaction against a decadent Scholasticism, was seized by a passion for the study of those languages in all their purity, and for the knowledge of their literary and philosophical masterpieces. The intellectual climate of Europe was transformed, as it were, overnight. Scholasticism, already seriously affected, declined still further, and the doctrinal teaching of the Church, with which Scholasticism was so closely associated, also suffered in prestige.

Along with either indifference or implied opposition to Catholic doctrines, the New Learning attacked the ascetical teaching of the Church and sapped the foundations of Christian morality. The literature of Greece and Rome, and such specimens of their sculpture and painting as had survived, described in all their variety and depth the emotions and passions of man—*quidquid agunt homines* ("the full range of human activity")—love, hatred, ambition, scorn—with the most consummate mastery of language. It was the cult of man in all his nakedness, and the total "amorality" which it bred entered into the ranks not only of the lay people but also of the higher clergy and of the papal court itself, who prided themselves on being patrons of the New Learning. This was the new type of humanism which the Church had to face; and she had either to bring it into harmony with her teaching or perish from it.

We have used the word *humanism* in speaking of the Catholic synthesis of the thirteenth century and in particular of the contribution made to it by the Dominican thinkers and the Franciscan preachers. That was a humanism which was integrated within the Christian system and included a vision of the divinization of man through the Incarnation and the life of grace. Christian morality and asceticism, quite distinct from the pessimism of Manichaeism and other Oriental cults, had its legitimate place in this humanism. It could include the cult of poverty also, because the Franciscans, who were the most authentic exponents of this humanism, were passionate devotees of poverty, by means of which they strove to imitate Our Lord more perfectly and to demonstrate the nobility of freedom from the passion of material gain and bodily comfort. Being sure of not underestimating the claims of the soul, they could, with greater freedom and spiritual insight, admire the world of nature and the beauties of the material universe and love them as expressions of the infinite perfections of God and as instruments of his benevolence towards men.

It is worth while to ask ourselves why such a vision of the physical aspects of nature and of man, implicit in Christianity, had not come to the Christian mind in earlier epochs. The reason certainly was the dualism of the Manichean system, which found echoes even in orthodox Christian minds. It influenced their understanding of the doctrine of the Fall and of original sin and the corruption of human nature. Some sentences of St. Paul, and many passages in St. Augustine, taken by themselves, encouraged this pessimism. Then again, the Patristic view of the physical world was not based on a realistic appreciation of the positive and intrinsic worth of the material universe, but on its allegoric significance, on its being the shadow and symbol of invisible realities. It was through the Thomistic theory of knowledge as abstraction from the data of sense experience that physical and material realities were understood and appreciated for what they were in themselves.

This philosophical development coincided with an important stage in the evolution in the ascetical outlook of the Church. The corruption and unbridled sensuality of decadent Roman life had created in the minds of the Christians of the primitive Church a horror of all bodily indulgence, even when legitimate, and a stern determination not to permit themselves any satisfaction which might resemble remotely the abominations of the pagans. A long period of mortification and abstinence was needed to purify for the Christian conscience the visage of the material world. The Church and the Christian people had to pass through those "centuries of Lent" before they could come to the paschal joys which the Franciscan revival symbolized. If the new humanism of the sixteenth century had understood the spirit and respected the limits of this earlier Christian humanism, there might have not only been no great harm done but there might have occurred a positive widening and deepening of the concept of humanism. But this is not what happened in the revival of learning; it was rather a return to man in all the force and violence of his untamed passions, but passions expressed with refinement of language and perfection of form. "How beauteous mankind is," exclaims Miranda in the *Tempest*. "O brave new world that has such creatures in it." But it was a beauty which made an abstraction of the laws of God and of the spiritual heights to which the soul of man was called, for "man", in the full worldly sense, was to be the measure of all things.

The tragedy was that the popes and churchmen were the most active and the most munificent patrons of this New Learning. Probably Nicholas V, the first of the Renaissance popes, did not see all the moral consequences of the new spirit; neither did he suspect the explosive power of the theories and examples of unqualified freedom of thought and action in which Greek literature and history abounded. This could not but work against a system whose mission was to safeguard the place of divinely constituted authority in the interpretation of Scripture and in the government of the people of God. The successors of Nicholas allowed the papal court, already weakened by the decay of Christian faith and morality, to be sullied with the immorality which was swamping the world of the Renaissance. Thus, we have the heartbreaking sight of a series of Renaissance popes who, far from continuing the work of reform begun by Martin V, became the most insurmountable obstacles to it. It was the return to that pagan licentiousness from which the primitive Christians had recoiled with horror.

In these conditions of weakened faith and moral decadence, the Protestant challenge was delivered, and the voice of Luther rang across Europe denouncing the papacy and rejecting fundamental points of Catholic doctrine and Church government. Luther was a typical product of his age. His mental outlook was dominated by the Nominalist rejection of the objective nature of abstract truth. He could not therefore accept the idea of faith as an intellectual adhesion to clearly formulated dogmas. He conceived it as a subjective persuasion of being saved by the grace of God in spite of the incurable corruption of human nature. Those who had this perfect inner persuasion did not need to be disturbed by the thought of their inevitable human weaknesses. In this way Luther forcefully reconciled the pessimistic view of human nature with the "humanistic" morality of the Renaissance. With such a concept of faith and justification, he could challenge the entire dogmatic and sacramental system of the Church.

The reigning pope, Leo X, a typical Renaissance prelate absorbed in the political cares of the Papal States and in the alliances and manoeuverings which they entailed, and intent on the social and cultural activities of the papal court—as also in promoting the fortunes of his family—scarcely realized the gravity of the Lutheran challenge. The usual repressive measures were taken, and Luther was invited to submit. When he refused to do so, he was excommunicated. But the German princes supported and protected him. In a short time the revolt spread over a great part of northern Germany and the Scandinavian countries. England followed, though for different reasons and pursuing a different religious line. The powerful genius of Calvin now joined in the attack and carried the principles of the Lutheran revolt to their logical conclusions. A great part of the Netherlands and of Switzerland was lost, and France and northern Italy were threatened. At last the papacy woke up to the disaster and, under Pope Paul III, took up in earnest the task of reform.

The nature and extent of that reform can be adequately summed up by saying that it consisted in the convocation and proceedings of the Council of Trent and in executing the Council's decrees. First came the formulation of Catholic teaching in the face of the Protestant innovations: the decrees on faith and justification; the Sacraments, and specially the Eucharist; on the cult of the Blessed Virgin and the saints; on purgatory; and on the primacy of Peter. Then came the promulgation and application of the disciplinary decrees which involved a thorough reform of the higher and the lower clergy, including the papal court. Within a period of sixty years, from 1530 to 1590, the great reforming popes, from Paul III to Sixtus V—including among them the fiery Carafa and the holy but inflexible Ghisleri (St. Pius V)—had completed a task which for centuries had been hoped and prayed for and which the papacy hitherto had seemed powerless to carry out effectively. Two powerful new orders helped the Church in this work of reconstruction, the Capuchins, and more particularly the Jesuits, with whose activities the great work of Catholic reconstruction, which is generally called the Counter-Reform, is associated.

From the point of view of our particular interest, what is to be noted in this new synthesis is the characteristically Catholic feature that it did not reject entirely the pagan humanism of the classical revival but accepted and assimilated it in the manner proper to the Church. The fundamental teachings of the Church on the nature and destiny of man, on the role of reason and its relation to faith, on the nature of the act of faith itself, were redefined with a new precision and clarity. With these safeguards the New Learning was not only accepted but made the ally of the Church inasmuch as the study of the classics became a part of Christian education and an instrument of intellectual training. The Jesuits became the foremost teachers of the classics in their schools, universities, and seminaries. The vast inner world of human emotion, which this literature laid open and developed, was brought into the service of religion and used for the cultivation of religious sentiment. There emerged what Bremond has called the "devout Humanism" of the post-Tridentine era, and a full description of this new piety will be found in the first volume of that author's monumental *Histoire du Sentiment Religieux en France*. I shall here choose only two examples to illustrate it. The first is the special type of "contemplation" which St. Ignatius Loyola taught in his *Spiritual Exercises*, a work which was one of the most efficacious instruments of the Catholic Reform. This contemplation consists in the devout evocation of the person and actions of Our Lord, "seeing the persons, hearing the words, and noting the actions." It aimed at an intimate knowledge of the mysteries of the life of Christ, from the

Incarnation to the Ascension, in all their concrete manifestations, and required that one dwell long and lovingly on every detail. Thus, Christ's sacred humanity becomes the model of Christian perfection. The fervent Christian's main effort should be to keep close to the God-Man, the leader and king, "to know him better, to love him more ardently, and to imitate him more closely." St. Ignatius, in keeping with his genius and objectives, gave an important place to the actions of Jesus in order to stir the exercitant to a life of zeal and apostolic effort. Obviously, this could not be done without attending also to the interior dispositions with which those actions were performed. (Perhaps St. Francis of Sales gave the finest literary expression to this humanistic ideal of Christian perfection in his two classics, *Introduction to the Devout Life* and *On the Love of God.*)

At a later stage of the Catholic Reform, another famous school of spirituality, known as the "Ecole Française" and founded in France by Bérulle, Olier, and Condren, paid more attention to the "interior" of Jesus, studying his life not so much through the external actions as by a consideration of the "states" of his mind. Their spirituality consists in teaching the Christian to reproduce those interior states. The Ignatian and the Berullian schools between them give an adequate idea of the direction which was given to Christian piety by the humanism of the Renaissance.

This special type of piety and religious devotion was sustained by the new schools of religious art, particularly architecture and painting, which are typical of the early Renaissance and of the post-Tridentine periods. After the prejudiced condemnation stemming from the modern "Gothic revival," Renaissance architecture, and even the much abused Baroque, is coming to be recognized as "the architecture of humanism," as the external expression of religious emotion which had become a part of the life and spirit of a triumphant Church.

Two stages are distinguishable in the growth of this religious art. The first is more definitely classical, reflecting the serenity of the cult of beauty characteristic of Greek art. The best representatives of this period are Bramante, Michaelangelo, and Raphael. But with the Catholic Reform a new spirit comes over it, the spirit of a restless and trimphant ardour, the spirit which, as Menendez de Pelaya proudly says, "had kept back the Protestant tide within its northern dykes," and had helped to destroy the power of the Turk in the battle of Lepanto. It was that "spirit of conquest" which had regained for the Church many lost provinces in Europe, and had established flourishing Churches in America, Asia, and Africa. In architecture it brought in the fantastic riches of the Baroque style; in painting it emphasized themes on which attention had been focussed by Protestant denials—Our Lord in the Eucharist, the Blessed Virgin and her privileges, St. Peter and his primacy, the martyrdoms, the ecstasies and exultations of the saints. The new masters are Correggio, Dominichino, and Guercino, Bernini and Maderna, Ribera and Murillo, Rubens and Van Dyke. (One must read of the quality and variety of this new Christian art in the beautiful book of Émile Mâle, *L'Art Religieux après le Concile de Trente.*)

The greatest treasures of this period are to be found in the Vatican Museum, the Sistine Chapel, and in certain churches —St. Peter's, S. Maria Maggiore, S. Andrea del Valle, the Chiesa Nuova, where St. Philip Neri reposes, the Gesù, and S. Ignazio. The treasures of St. Peter's are inexhaustible. From crypt to cupola it is an epitome of the history of the Church, more particularly of the Catholic Reform: statues and mosaics recall the popes and saints who led the Reform and the doctrines which they vindicated. It contains every type of artistic expression from the pure graceful lines of Michaelangelo's *Pietà* to the riotous profusion of the *Glory* of Bernini, from the ethereal beauty of Raphael's transfigured Christ to the passionate and crowded canvasses of Domenichino. Byron's lines on St. Peter's are exact:

> But thou, of temples old or altars new
> Standst alone, with nothing like to thee.

No less important was the manner in which the Catholic Reform influenced European literature after the Renaissance. It was through the literature of Greece and Rome that the New Learning had come to Europe, and that literature acted as a powerful stimulus to the flowering of the modern European literature. The post-Renaissance literature of Italy, England, France, and Spain is among the supreme creative achievements of Europe. In those writings of infinite variety—romances, epics, dramas, and lyrics—it is man, in all the multiplicity of his attitudes and the complexities of his psychology, who is portrayed with extraordinary insight and power. The pagan inspiration of much of it in form and matter is obvious. But Christianity, and in particular the Catholic Revival, was able to capture the minds and hearts of some of the greatest of the writers, and some of the finest of their works have a decidedly Christian inspiration. I shall name only a few of them: in Italy, Tasso, with his great epic *Jerusalem Delivered;* in Spain, the profoundly religious dramas of Calderon; in France, almost at the end of the period of Catholic Reform and in the last period of his own troubled life, the two biblical dramas of Racine, *Esther* and *Athalie,* supreme examples of perfect classic art in the service of the Christian faith.[1]

---

[1] In *Athalie* there is a magnificent passage in which the High Priest Joad sees a vision of the glory of the future Church. Maurice Baring considered this one of the highest achievements of French poetry, and I quote the opening lines:

> *Quelle Jérusalem nouvelle*
> *Sort du fond du desert brillante de clartés*

Admittedly, however, the greatest writer of that age was Shakespeare. Putting aside the question of his personal beliefs,[2] I think that Shakespeare did express the Catholic mind to a large extent in all his works, and that *Macbeth* in particular is a drama whose central theme is Christian and treated in a Christian way. It is the study of a soul under temptation, freely choosing evil, enticed but not constrained thereto by mysterious influences which Macbeth finally recognizes to be the powers of hell; a soul reaching the last stage of moral degradation by repeated sin. He knows what has gone wrong with him; for worldly gain he has surrendered "his eternal jewel to the common enemy of man." An American critic, R. G. Moulton, has said that *Macbeth* is the most classical of Shakespeare's plays. It is also the most Christian. It is, I think, the perfect fusion of classical drama and the medieval morality play. It is a tragedy of character, not the tragedy of fate.

Protestantism, both Lutheran and Calvinist, had no love for humanism; for them, it was but the exhibition of human corruption. It is typical that in *Pilgrim's Progress*, which is a landmark in the evolution of Protestant culture, Bunyan should have gone back to the medieval device of the allegory to express the moral fervour of puritanism. Yet, Milton in *Comus* and *Lycidas* succeeded perfectly in fusing a classic love of beauty with the same moral fervour. *The Ode on the Nativity, Paradise Lost,* and *Paradise Regained,* not withstanding Milton's puritanism, are in many ways typical of Christian humanism. No one can read without profound emotion how the blind

---

Et porte sur le front une marque immortelle?
Peuples de la terre, chantez.
Jerusalem renait, plus brillante et plus belle.

(Act III, Sc. VII)

[2] I believe that the books of the Countess de Chambrun (an American non-Catholic) have made a fairly convincing case in favour of his fidelity to Catholicism.

poet, like his own Samson "fallen on evil days, in darkness compassed round and solitude," recalls the beauty of the world which he had never ceased to love:

> Thus with the year
> Seasons return, but not to me returns
> Day, or the sweet approach of ev'n or morn
> Or sight of vernal bloom or summer's rose,
> Or flocks or herds or human face divine.

It is a picture of the world and of man in which there is no discernible trace of Calvinist theology.

Another result of the influence of the new humanism was a keener realization of the political and social implications of the Christian concept of the dignity of man. Thus, such theologians as Bellarmine and Vázquez developed the doctrine of the "sovereignty of the peeople," and Suarez enunciated some of the basic principles of an international order. All this was in contrast to the absolutism of kings defended by Luther and by the Anglican theologians under James I. At the same time, there were new manifestations of the "social apostolate" more universal than the earlier and more specialized apostolate for the redemption of captives and the cure of the lepers —there were the vast undertakings of St. Vincent de Paul; the service of the sick by St. John of God and his Benefratelli; the passionate defence of the rights of the American Indians by Las Casas; the heroic work of St. Peter Claver for the Negro slaves in America.

We mentioned briefly the role of the saints in the Catholic Revival, and we have seen the part they played in the earlier stages of the history of the Church, from apostolic times down to such great popular preachers as St. Bernardine of Siena. The pre-Reformation saints were leaders and moral reformers, constructors of the "Christian city" in the world of pagans and barbarians. But with the saints of the Catholic Revival we see a more rounded perfection—a revelation of human qualities, a combination of holiness and active interest in the life and activity of the world which had not been seen before to the same extent. The very cult of the saints and their intercessory power had been challenged by Protestantism. A response to this is to be seen perhaps in the extraordinary flowering of heroic sanctity in this period. We find men who were saints and, at the same time, rulers, organizers, thinkers, writers—men who knew the world and were alert to the problems of life in the world, men who were "practical mystics" (that "most formidable combination of human qualities," as John Morley described it). There were saints on and near the papal throne, such as Pius V and Charles Borromeo. There were the great founders of religious orders and the men around them— Cajetan, Philip Neri, and Ignatius Loyola with the first Jesuit saints. There were great mystics who were also great reformers, such as Teresa of Avila and John of the Cross; theologians and writers, such as Bellarmine and Francis de Sales; servants of the poor, such as Vincent de Paul and Peter Claver; and saints in the flower of youth, such as Aloysius Gonzaga, John Berchmans, and Stanislaus Kostka.

In such men we see the place of supernatural sanctity in the Christian ideal of human perfection. The mystery of Jesus and of the Church, which was the starting point of our inquiry, is illustrated in them more perfectly than in any others. Through them we see how the entire person and all the activity of regenerated man can be brought under the rule of divine grace, and enlisted in the service of his Church in her continuous and ever-widening efforts to "restore all things in Christ."

CHAPTER V

THE CHURCH AND THE CIVILIZATIONS OF ASIA AND AMERICA

We have seen that the sixteenth century was a period of revolution which brought to Europe, and to the Church established for the greater part in Europe, a widening of boundaries and an opening of new horizons. We have considered that widening in the intellectual and artistic spheres through the Renaissance and in the cultural consequences of the Protestant revolt. It was obviously more a widening of horizons than of boundaries. We must now consider the encounter of the Church with the peoples and civilizations of America and Asia, which constituted both a widening of boundaries in the physical sense and also of an enlarging of intellectual vision. This latter phenomenon was brought about mainly through the discovery of Chinese wisdom and Hindu religious thought and sentiment. The full consequences of this encounter of Europe and of the Church with the achievements of the Asian mind are not yet fully apparent. But they may, in the long run, be at least as important and as far-reaching as the rediscovery of Greek and Latin letters and as the New Learning which resulted from it.

Contacts between Christian Europe and Asia—both India and China—had existed before the sixteenth century, but they were made for the greater part either by travellers like Marco Polo or by merchants who sought the silks of China and the spices of India. For the rest, Europe looked upon them and on Africa as the vast pagan world, the "Gentiles" as opposed to the "chosen people" (as the Christians of Europe regarded themselves, being forgetful of the time when they were themselves "Gentiles"). No far-reaching movement of conversion was made among them, since, among other reasons, the overland path of the Europeans to Asia was blocked by their traditional and victorious Muslim adversaries: Arabs, Moors, and Turks. But the triumph of the Catholic Revival and the impetuous zeal for the extension of the Church which it created could not but turn the attention of the Catholic apostles to the East. The discovery of the route to India round the Cape of Good Hope, and the mastery of the seas secured for Portugal by the genius of Henry the Navigator, gave to these apostles of the Catholic Reform the possibility of reaching the fabled countries of Asia without being stopped by the Muslims.

Once the way was opened, the adventurous spirit of sixteenth-century Portugal and Spain, with its ardent anti-Muslim passion, led them to penetrate into the farthest recesses of Asia in order to halt the Muslim advance and to establish their own maritime and commercial power there. At the same time, they shared the apostolic spirit which the Catholic Revival had engendered and were animated by a zeal for the conversion of non-Christian people. We see, therefore, the pioneers and builders of the Spanish and Portuguese empires in the forefront of the missionary enterprise of the sixteenth and seventeenth centuries. The soldier and the administrator were always accompanied by the priest and the preacher. Though the indifference, the cupidity, and the cruelty of the colonizers and conquerors often compromised the mission of the Church, the rulers themselves never wavered in their determination to be the instruments of God for the extension of the Church, its patrons, and protectors wherever they established their rule. Of the growth of the Church in America we shall say something further on, but first let us consider what is more important from our point of view—the effort to evan-

gelize the people of the ancient civilizations of Asia in China,
Japan, and India.

In this Asian enterprise the greatest figure is that of St.
Francis Xavier. He went to the East on the invitation and under
the protection of the king of Portugal. He accomplished there
a work of vast proportions and left Christian communities in
India, Indonesia, Malaya, and Japan. There seemed at first
to be every chance of these beginnings developing into wider
movements of conversion to Christianity. But these hopes were
not fulfilled, for, a few years after the death of St. Francis, the
conversions almost everywhere diminished and the missionary
work languished. This was due in part to the scandalous life
of the Europeans resident in Asia—administrators, soldiers, and
merchants—but a deeper reason was a defect in the method
of evangelization, which St. Francis Xavier had not been able
to foresee and forestall.

The growing nationalism of the European countries had both
a political and a cultural aspect. Politically, it led to jealousy
among nations and the desire to exclude "foreigners" from the
privileges enjoyed by one's own nation. This was extended to
the religious sphere also; thus, the Spanish and Portuguese not
only asked the pope—Alexander VI as it happened—to divide
the world between the two and exclude the activity of one
in the sphere of the other as regards colonization; they also
decided that the missionaries of one country should not work
in the territory of the other. Because of the position of patronage enjoyed by secular rulers in the Church, the conversion
of the people of non-European countries and their admission
into the Church acquired a political colour. This type of religious patronage, accepted, and indeed beneficial, at the beginning, was to do harm to the missionary apostolate of the
Church in more recent times and up to this day.

Again this same nationalism, at first instinctively and un-
consciously, affected the very method of evangelization; it led

to a mode of integrating the converts within the body of the Church which, in the long run, was disastrous. The missionaries took it for granted that one could not be a Catholic without being like themselves—i.e., Spanish or Portuguese—in every particular, in doctrinal beliefs and in the external ways of life. So the converts were asked to accept at baptism not only a personal saint's name, but also a family name, one or other of those common in Spain and Portugal. The one selected was generally that of the godparents.[1] The neophytes were encouraged to dress like the Europeans, to eat and drink in the European manner. The churches were built after the European model, generally in a pseudo-Baroque style of doubtful taste. The vestments, the pictures and the statues, the music, and almost all other external manifestations of devotion, such as processions and pilgrimages, the confraternities and their insignia, were faithful reproductions of what was being done in the mother country. The converts were even encouraged to give up their languages and make their confessions in Portuguese or Spanish. The Europeans of that generation could not conceive of a Catholicism which was not "dressed up" in the particular style of their own civilization.

It is therefore not surprising that in India and Japan the converts formed a separate and isolated community, despised and mistrusted by the better classes, or that the attempts of the missionaries of Macao to penetrate into China—whose people considered the rest of the world to be barbarians—were fruitless. The Church had not been properly "planted" in these regions, and consequently she was not striking roots there and not gaining the strength needed to grow and spread out and weather the storms that were sure to beat on her before long.

[1] This explains such surnames as Fernandez, De Souza, Pinto, Diaz, etc., among several groups of Catholics in Asia who are racially pure Asians.

It was Alessandro Valignano, one of the greatest of the successors of St. Francis Xavier in the East, who first perceived the error of this method and set about to correct it. He may be justly described as the great organizer who took in hand and consolidated the pioneering achievements of St. Francis Xavier. He was sent to the East as visitor to all the Jesuit missions. He spent four years in Goa, and saw the defects of the system followed there. He encouraged the study of Indian languages and established a school for this purpose. Then he went to Macao as visitor of the Japanese mission and resided there for twenty-five years, going to Japan on three crucial occasions and staying there long enough to initiate new policies in order to overcome crises which had arisen. His great influence with two of the makers of modern Japan, the *shoguns* Nobunaga and Hideyoshi, enabled him to promote the interests of the missions effectively and, on more than one occasion, either to prevent or to stop serious persecution of the Christians.

Valignano saw quite clearly that the missions in Japan could not be established by the force and prestige of the European nations, as it had been in the territories which had become the colonies of Spain and Portugal. In Japan and China, the Church had to be built from the outset on the love and attachment of the people of the country. This called for a local clergy and for the adoption of external forms of worship in conformity with the traditions and culture of the land. Valignano loved and admired intensely the Japanese people, so he started schools for the study of Japanese and seminaries for the training of Japanese priests. He encouraged Japanese art, painting, and sculpture. This was the beginning of the method of "adaptation" of Asian culture to the expression of the Christian faith and the necessities of Christian practice. By this system, and by the success of the missionaries in converting the *daimyo*, or feudal nobles, who had great influence over their retainers, the conversion of Japan proceeded at a very rapid pace.

But there was one danger to the missions which Valignano had foreseen but could not impede. He did not want Japan to be the scene of rivalry between missionaries of the different nations and different religious orders. In particular, he opposed the coming of Spanish missionaries there because the political rivalry between Spain and Portugal would lead the suspicious Japanese leaders to see political implications in missionary work. This is exactly what happened when Spanish missionaries of different orders did get into Japan. Ieyasu, the masterful founder of the Tokugawa Shogunate, thought that the final result of Christian penetration into Japan would be—as had happened in the Philippines—the conquest of the country. He started the cruel persecution of the Christians in 1616 with a ruthlessness which all but stamped out Japanese Christianity. Valignano had died in 1606, but if his views had prevailed this disaster to Catholicism might have been avoided.[2]

But Valignano's work was not limited to Japan. He had a great admiration for the Chinese as a people who, unlike all other nations, were ruled not by soldiers but by scholars. The authority of the ruling class was based on their knowledge of the Chinese classics and their understanding of the wisdom of their ancestors. So he had appointed Michael Ruggieri to study the Chinese language and, through the gateway of Macao, to seek admission into the hitherto forbidden territory of the Chinese Empire. Ruggieri, however, was not adept at learning languages, so Valignano gave him as companion another Italian priest whom he had known in Rome and who

[2] There is no need for me to recount here the miraculous survival of a handful of Japanese Catholics in the remoter islands and hiding places around Nagasaki, and their dramatic discovery and restoration to active communion with the Church in the nineteenth century by the fathers of the Paris Foreign Missions.

had early chosen the Eastern missions. This was Matteo Ricci, who had a first-rate memory and a great aptitude for languages. He had been a student of the famous Clavius in the Roman College, and was, among other things, an excellent mathematician and astronomer. These were just the qualifications likely to impress the Chinese, who admired learning above all else and who had enormous respect for "wise men."

Ricci set himself the difficult task, not only of learning the language, but mastering the classics and entering into the very spirit of the people whom he had made his own. It took him ten long years to gain entry into the circles of scholars and nobles, first in Nanking and then in Pekin. He made himself first of all respected and acceptable to the Chinese as being truly learned, in some ways more learned than their own scholars. It was only after this that he began preaching the faith—and then he presented the Christian doctrines in terms intelligible and pleasing to cultured Chinese.

Soon the Chinese saw that Ricci's knowledge of the Chinese classics and mastery of the Chinese ideograms was greater even than that of the Mandarins. The priest had at first dressed himself as a Buddhist bonze, but he found that this did not bring him the respect of the learned circles and so he dressed himself as a scholar and imitated in every detail the elaborate manners of the learned class. Over and above this he had what the Mandarins did not have: a mastery of astronomy, the ability to make and repair clocks, and a talent for mapmaking. Soon he had around him a group of fervent admirers to whom he could present Christian doctrine with a chance of being heard with respect.

Ricci realized that it would not be possible to convert the Chinese if he represented Christianity in an entirely alien garb and as wholly different from the moral teaching of the Chinese classics. He saw that the basic doctrines accepted in Confucianism were in harmony with Christianity. It was an ethical system concerned mainly with social organization and family life in which piety to ancestors was an essential feature. It also had a theistic basis in which God was referred to as the Lord of Heaven or simply as Heaven. Its moral teaching was noble and fostered unequivocally the best natural virtues. Ricci thus could present Christianity as a crown and completion of the teaching of Confucius. He also found that opposition to the doctrines of Buddhism, though it stirred to anger the bonzes, did not prejudice him in the eyes of the nobles and scholars.

He translated the commandments and the Creed into Chinese, and proceeded to expound Christian doctrine in several works of literary excellence which are now considered to be valuable contributions to Chinese literature. Among them we may mention the *Disputation about God* (against the Buddhists), *Twenty-Five Sentences* (a summary of Christian doctrine), and *Ten Paradoxes,* a book of moral teachings based on the Christian revelation.

One particularly important decision of Ricci, made with the approval of Valignano, was to have far-reaching consequences; he had examined carefully the honours paid to the dead and to the spirits of ancestors in Chinese family life, and came to the conclusion that they were not essentially divine honours but such as were paid also to distinguished living people. So, while he rigorously excluded everything really superstitious in Chinese funeral customs, he allowed converts to retain such practices as the ceremonious bowing before the images or statues of their ancestors. This enabled him to get over one of the major obstacles to the conversion of the Chinese. Before he died he had around him a group of devoted and distinguished converts, and he could say to his disciples and successors, "I leave to you the open door."

In fact the conversion of the best elements in Chinese life proceeded rapidly under the successors of Ricci. The story of the opposition to his methods and the failure of the great experiment to convert the entire empire to the faith will be touched upon later. It is enough to note here the greatness of the man and the far-reaching implications of his work. Arnold Toynbee, in *The World and the West*, calls him "one of the greatest of modern missionaries and modern scholars," and compares his work of harmonizing Chinese wisdom and Christianity to that of Origen and Clement of Alexandria in harmonizing Greek philosophy and Christianity.

We must now turn our attention to another and not less significant example of adaptation, Robert de Nobili's attempt to Christianize Hindu thought and Hindu social and religious practices. De Nobili was much younger than Ricci. He owed much to Ricci's experiences in China. Moreover, Valignano had spent some time in Goa and had seen that the Europeanizing method of the earlier missionaries had ended in failure. He had tried to promote the study of Indian languages and to encourage Indian vocations to the priesthood. Thus, the attempt of De Nobili, like that of Ricci, was due in large measure to the vision and initiative of Valignano.

The religious conditions in India were far more complex than those of China. There a group of Christians of the Oriental Rite (descendants of the converts of St. Thomas according to ancient tradition), had remained faithful to their Syrian Rite and socially were well integrated with the rest of Indian society. The early European missionaries, however, had looked upon them with mistrust and tried to make them adopt the Latin Rite and Latin forms of worship, but most of them remained faithful to their traditions and today form an important and flourishing section of the Oriental Church in communion with Rome. The sixteenth-century missionaries left them aside as an isolated group and began the evangelization of India as if it were a new movement and not a continuation of the earlier wave of conversions. These new converts were, as I said, led to adopt European ways of living, and this included such practices as the eating of beef and the drinking of alcoholic beverages, which the higher castes in India regarded with repugnance. Because of these habits, the Feringhees, as the "Franks" or Europeans were known, were looked upon socially as little better than the lowest rank in Indian society, the outcasts or untouchables.

In spite of this, the manifest holiness of St. Francis Xavier brought thousands of genuine converts even from the better classes. And St. Francis himself had clear ideas of how the Church was to be planted in India. He encouraged the education of Indian youth and the encouragement of vocations. But after him the flow of conversions thinned and then practically stopped. Then, in conformity with the spirit of those times of fierce intolerance in Europe, force was used by the Portuguese to obtain conversions. The Inquisition of Goa earned an unenviable reputation for severity. It was this condition which Robert de Nobili wanted to change.

De Nobili realized that, unless some allowance were made for the social conventions and cultural traditions of India, the country would not be converted. He saw the fatal mistake of beginning the instruction of a would-be convert with the question: "Do you wish to embrace the Feringhee religion?" To find out which of the customs were definitely religious and superstitious in character, and which were purely civil, he had to study Indian religious thought and literature. He very quickly saw that the superstitions of the masses and the popular idolatry were far from being the whole truth about Indian religion. It must be admitted that Francis Xavier himself did not see much more than this superstition, and the pride and deceitfulness of the Brahmans. His judgement on Indian religion is severe. It is worth reproducing a few words of Father Broderick on this subject:

St. Francis knew next to nothing of the real India, no
more than did any of his European contemporaries. . . .
The mystery and majesty of India eluded him altogether.
He, the man of uttermost prayer, never guessed that he
was in the most religious land in the world, a land which
taught countless millions of men to pray, Chinese and
Japanese no less than Hindus. How tawdry and insignifi-
cant the brief histories and imperial ambitions of Spain,
France, Holland and England appear when set over
India's three thousand years of ceaseless passionate search
for the eternal and the divine. The gross superstitions and popular idolatry which St. Francis witnesses
are not, as he seemed to think, the whole of the story,
but its least significant part; and, all aberrations considered, it seems true of India as it was true of Francis himself, that God was its entire adventure. If he could have
met his great contemporary in Northern India, the poet
of Bhakti or tender devotion, Tulsi Das, he would have
revised his views of Indian religion.[3]

Now Robert de Nobili resolved to study what Francis Xavier
had neither the time nor, given the circumstances, the incen-
tive to do. De Nobili studied Sanscrit, perhaps the first modern European to do so; he studied also Tamil and Telugu, the
principal languages of the south, both rich in literature. He
spent years in poring over the authentic Hindu religious texts.
Imitating Ricci in China, he put on the dress of the Hindu
ascetic, the *sanyasin*—the ochre-coloured garments and the
wooden sandals. He lived their very abstemious and mortified
life: no meat, no alcoholic drink. Up to a certain point he accepted and observed the distinctions of caste. He did not eat
with the untouchable class, he carried the sacred thread of the
"twice born" after blessing it as he would have blessed a scapu-

[3] *Life of St. Francis Xavier*, pp. 326, 327.

lar. Since he was a priest and a nobleman in his own country, he called himself a "Brahman"—a Jesuit Brahman. Living in a typical hermitage in the manner of a Hindu *guru* or religious teacher, he could gather disciples around him and discuss with the Hindu scholars with more than the learning of the ordinary Brahman.

This brought De Nobili, who came to be known as Tattva-bhodakar, the "Preacher of Truth," a large number of "disciples" from among the higher castes of the south and many converts among them. He allowed them to retain some of the practices of their caste—their choice of food and ways of serving and eating; the wearing of the sacred thread, the use of the *tilak* on the forehead and of sandal paste on the body, the daily "ritual" bath, etc. He gave them prayers and hymns in their own language and did away with the custom of teaching them Portuguese and imposing Portuguese names upon them. In the purely religious sphere he introduced one change which was to have consequences exactly like those which were caused by the honours to the dead which Ricci had permitted to his converts. De Nobili, knowing the unconquerable repugnance of the Hindu to touch the saliva of another person, decided that in the baptismal rite the *epphetha* could be omitted. With these adaptations and innovations De Nobili began to receive converts from the higher castes in increasing numbers.

But the battle was not won without further and bitter struggles. The older school of missionaries, at least many of them, were in genuine doubt about the prudence and even the orthodoxy of some of the customs he had tolerated. They were also wounded in their national "pride and prejudice" by the indifference to Portuguese ways and by the respect shown to the customs and manners of a pagan people. Angry petitions and protestations went to Rome. De Nobili was summoned to Goa by Archbishop de Sa, who had come from Portugal with the express purpose of putting an end to the "scandal of Madura."

But the Jesuit superiors of De Nobili and Cardinal Bellarmine in Rome defended him. De Nobili himself wrote a brilliant apology justifying his method by the example of the Christian Church from the time of Gregory the Great, who had approved of just such adaptations when converting the barbarians of Europe. Finally Pope Gregory XV, in 1623, approved the method, and his words are worth quoting from the brief *Romanae Sedis antistites:*

> Taking into consideration human weakness as much as it is permissible without sin and without scandal, desirous to favour the conversion of those peoples who do not wish to give up the tuft of hair, the cord, the baths, the sandal paste which indicated their nobility of caste and office, and after diligent study and discussion . . . by Our Apostolic authority we allow, to the Brahmans and others to be converted, the use of the cord and the tuft of hair. . . . The sandal paste which is an ornament of the body is further permitted, and so are the baths for health and cleanliness.

De Nobili had won his battle. As in China, so in India, the door was now open and the conversion of the most genuine representatives of the two most ancient civilizations of Asia was now possible. The Christianizing of those cultures was well on its way.

Ricci and De Nobili were the most remarkable Europeans who went to the East—men of the highest intelligence, of indomitable will, and of exceptional religious virtue and spirit of sacrifice. The knowledge of the East which they took to Europe—the wisdom of China and the philosophy and religious speculations of India—had their effect on the cultural development of Europe, similar in its way to the effect of the New Learning. The process, however, is not yet complete. As we shall see, even today the assimilation of Eastern thought by

Christian doctrine and culture claims the attention of Catholic thinkers and scholars and holds out exciting possibilities. For the present we shall conclude this brief review of the work of the Tattvabhodakar with this judgement of a Protestant scholar, Mr. P. Thomas, who says (pp. 72 and 76) in his *Christians and Christianity in India and Pakistan:*

> It should not be imagined that Fr. Robert adopted his way of life out of sheer hypocrisy. He loved it. He was something of an ascetic and believed that a meagre vegetarian diet and strictness of personal habits was in conformity with the higher life. He became an Indian to save the Indians even as God became man to save mankind and there was nothing demeaning or irreligious about that. While he gave up his nationality for India, De Nobili certainly did not give up his religion. . . . In his deep insight into human nature, his sympathy with Indian culture and traditions, in his recognition of the prophetic presage of the Indian sages of the coming of the Saviour, he stands alone among the Europeans of his time who were inclined to treat the Hindus as a God-forsaken set of idolaters.

Before closing this chapter, I should say a few words about Africa and America. The encounter of the Church with the non-Christian cultures of these continents is not so well documented as the meeting between "East and West" which took place in China and India. Nor were there in these great regions cultures as advanced as in Asia; but it would be a mistake to underestimate those that did exist. Before the slave raids in modern times by Arabs and Europeans had almost destroyed the manhood of Africa, there were flourishing kingdoms there, and tribal cultures with religious and ethical elements capable of being assimilated in the way proper to the Church. We know that they are being studied and utilized now by the modern African Church. But in the sixteenth and seventeenth centuries, the Portuguese and Spaniards, intent upon their more exciting enterprises in Asia and America, had not the men or the energy to cultivate these fields assiduously. They did, however, make efforts in two directions. First they established mission stations in the coastal countries along which they sailed both in the west and the east: in Guinea, at the Cape in the extreme south, in Mozambique, in Mombasa, and in Madagascar. The Jesuits, the Capuchins, and the Augustinians worked in these territories. The missionaries penetrated into the eastern Congo also, and there the conversion of a king who was baptized under the name of Alfonso stirred hopes in Europe of a new Constantine leading Africa to the Faith.[4] But these missions made little progress. Many of the converts later embraced, or reverted to, Islam.

A second line of missionary effort in Africa was work among the Copts of Egypt and Ethiopia, all strongly attached to Monophysism. St. Ignatius had sent Father Oviedo to Ethiopia. He had no great success. At a later stage the conversion of one of the kings raised high hopes, but here, too, it was a false start and Monophysism returned soon with greater intolerance. The attempt to convert the Copts of Egypt was not more successful. The glorious African Church of Cyprian, Augustine, and Tertullian had passed away, leaving hardly a trace. The period of the Catholic Reform passed, too, without achieving notable success in Africa. The hour of grace had not yet struck. It was to come four centuries later to usher in the astonishing Pentecostal diffusion of the Church which we see today in Africa.

[4] There is a reference to this conversion in the statue of the African king in the marble group by Theoudon to the left of the altar of St. Ignatius in the Gesù: *The Triumph of Faith over Paganism*. To the left is the magnificent group of Legros' *Religion Strikes Down Heresy*. Legros was a convert from Protestantism.

In America the Christian conquerors did encounter, particularly in Central and South America, some highly developed civilizations. The fact that they have not survived the European occupation in the way that the Asian civilizations have has led to the general impression that they were almost entirely destroyed. This indeed was the case with the Indians of North America, but such an impression would be erroneous in other instances. The Spanish Conquistadores were certainly cruel and rapacious, but they had, like most Latin people, a deeper sense of human equality and dignity than the northern nations, which exterminated the natives more or less systematically. The Spaniards did not resort to such destruction. There are today wide areas in the highlands of Mexico, Central America, Colombia, Ecuador, Perù, and Bolivia where the Indians could live, and continue to live, retaining most of their traditional ways though most of them are Christians by faith. The conquerors also intermarried with the natives, and started a movement of racial assimilation which might have created everywhere in these lands well-integrated nations with much greater political and social stability. But the movement was arrested by certain obstacles.

The first obstacle was the introduction of African slaves and the consequent irruption among all the lower classes of superstitions and social abuses which have caused deterioration in the physical and cultural standards of the Indians. Then came the suppression of the Society of Jesus and the weakening of the missionary and civilizing work of the Church. Finally, there were the wars of independence against Spain and the consequent opposition to Spain and all her policies—which included assimilation of the Indian races. The vacuum created by the departure of the Spaniards was filled, at least in the economic sphere, by the English and the Americans. Their example has helped to foster the spirit of separatism and class superiority on the part of the ruling class. That is why the gulf between the Indians and the Spanish-Americans is still very wide.

All this notwithstanding, it is clear that in the religious sphere some degree of adaptation was achieved. Traditional celebrations of Indian festivals were skilfully combined with Christian feasts. The dances and allegorical representations of native inspiration were brought in on the feasts of Our Lady and the great annual celebrations of Corpus Christi. Indian skill in construction and decoration was used in some of the churches in South America, which are among the most gorgeous Baroque edifices in the world. Today there is a revival of Indian culture in the countries which I have mentioned above. There is little doubt that the type of "adaptation" which the Church will foster in the changed conditions of the twentieth century will take into account this revived Indian culture of Mexico and Central and South America.[5]

I admit that some of these statements are conjectural. But on one point at least we are on solid ground: the defence of the rights of the Indians by churchmen against the cruelties and injustices of the European colonists. It is in refreshing contrast to the general indifference to their welfare. Bartholomew Las Casas and his passionate denunciations before the kings of Spain of the wrongs the Indians suffered is one great example. Another, and more original, was the attempt of the Jesuits to keep them from molestation in the Reductions of Paraguay and to give them a way of life in conformity with their character and inclinations. (This fascinating story may be read in the book of a brilliant non-Catholic writer R. B. Cunninghame Graham, *A Vanished Arcadia.*) The greatest adversaries of the Jesuits, men like Voltaire and D'Alembert, have paid tributes to the work of the Church and of the Society of Jesus in setting up these Reductions. They saved the Indians of many genera-

[5] I am indebted to a South American colleague for these details.

tions from the cruelty of their European masters and the callousness of the slave drivers, though all this was swept away later with the suppression of the society. But it is impossible not to pause before this truly Catholic enterprise and not to feel a passionate regret at the thought of what was and what might have been.

CHAPTER VI

FROM THE CATHOLIC REVIVAL
TO THE REVOLUTION

The sixteenth-century Catholic Revival and the reconstruction which it had brought about with apparently such complete success had been carried out in a world-wide setting characteristic of the modern age. It had taken cognizance of the religious and cultural changes in Europe and confronted the ancient civilizations and deep-rooted religions of Asia as well as the more primitive ways and beliefs of the original inhabitants of America and Africa. The Church had defined her attitude and determined her policy towards all of them. These events and developments had given her actions a world-wide dimension for the first time. It marked, at least in its essence, the culmination of her expansion in widening circles, beginning with the Judaeo-Hellenic world of her first beginnings, the Greco-Roman and Latino-Byzantine world of the Roman Empire, then Europe with its many emerging nationalities, and finally the world scene of the modern age.

Throughout these vicissitudes and changes of external circumstances she had remained herself, conscious of her identity and changeless in her doctrine; changeless, however, in a special sense, namely in retaining unchanged the inner core of her teaching but at the same time, by virtue of its dynamic quality, admitting extensions and enrichments through a logical and coherent development of that inner core. This is true for her dogmas. It is also true—and that is the theme of this essay—of that corpus of essential doctrines and principles, taught by reason or deduced from revealed supernatural truth, with which she informs and inspires the civilizations by which man organizes his social life and constructs his terrestrial "city." Because of this law of growth and development, she has widened and enriched the core of essential principles at each important stage of her pilgrimage on earth and thus carried to the next stage, to her encounter with a wider group, a larger corpus of what we may call her "secular doctrines."

Since the Catholic Revival and expansion of the Church in the sixteenth century had brought her face to face with most of the peoples of the world, it might have been thought that the cultural synthesis and the politico-social situation which resulted from that confrontation would be relatively enduring, or at least more so than the earlier constructions. In reality, however, the new order was in some ways more short-lived than the preceding ones. In less than two hundred years, opposition and revolts, reaction and regression, plunged the Church into one of her most dangerous crises and threatened her very existence.

For all the magnificence of the external triumph of the Church after the Tridentine Reform, there were in Catholic Europe currents of thought and ways of life which were out of harmony with the genuine Catholic spirit and which were calculated to corrode the better elements. The pagan humanism of the classical revival had been, it is true, Christianized and made to serve piety and devotion and charity. But the instincts of the natural man which it had stirred up and encouraged were never completely brought back under control. Even in the best Catholic circles, there was a love of pleasure and a delight in purely sensuous beauty which was fundamentally pagan. The art of Christian and Catholic Europe tended to be amoral, if not openly immoral. This bred opposition to the restraining influence of Catholic moral and ascetical teaching, and an inclination to throw off the spiritual authority and doctrinal teaching of the Church.

A deeper malady was the slow but almost irresistible growth of unbelief. There are unbelievers and atheists in any society and at all periods.[1] But in the seventeenth and eighteenth centuries their number in Catholic countries, and particularly in France, increased in alarming proportions, and they began to occupy places of importance in the cultural life of the country. France had been in the forefront of the Catholic Revival, giving to the post-Tridentine Church a galaxy of saints, theologians, and devotional writers unequalled in any country. We have to think only of St. Francis of Sales and St. Vincent de Paul, of Bérulle and Olier and Condren, of St. Jeanne Frances de Chantal and St. Louise de Marillac to be convinced of this. In cultural matters, the prestige of France was supreme in all Europe. When, therefore, unbelief spread among the French intellectuals and some of the most gifted men of the country became scoffers and atheists, the effect on the rest of Catholic Europe was harmful in the extreme.

Many currents fed this spirit of unbelief in France. There was the example given by the freedom of speculation and indifference to authority which Greek and Latin literature, even in its bowdlerized and carefully annotated editions, could not hide from the youth of Europe. Then, in Protestant countries where the Thomistic reconciliation of reason and faith was either ignored or made little of, there developed a merely natural theology. The rejection of authority in religion and the right of private judgement led first to diversities of interpretation of Scripture and then to total scepticism. The Protestant countries, specially England and Holland, saw the rise of

[1] It will interest the reader to know that even in the intensely and fundamentally religious culture of Hindu India, room was found for the negative and atheistic schools of the Charvakas and Nastikas.

Deism, a religion of rational thought and natural virtues which rejected the supernatural elements of revealed religion. It became the creed of most of the educated classes.

In France the Deists and Atheists—Voltaire, Rousseau, D'Alembert, and others—had two powerful weapons to disseminate their unbelief. They were men of literary genius; their wit and brilliance of style enabled them to captivate the masses.[2] Secondly, through the *Encyclopedia* they popularized knowledge, and presented it to the common people from an openly rationalistic point of view. Moreover, in their avowed object of destroying the Church and all religious belief, they were aided by two movements within the Church itself, movements which greatly weakened her power of resistance to unbelief: Gallicanism, and Jansenism.

Gallicanism is the name applied to the movement which was designed to make the Church of France virtually independent of the Roman pontiffs and, consequently, dependent upon the French kings. It had its origins in a combination of the old Catholic system of alliance between church and state and the new current of nationalism which was sweeping over Europe in the seventeenth century. We have noted from the time of Constantine the role of the emperors as the protectors and patrons of the Church. This had given many advantages to the Church, first in the task of converting the nations and then in consolidating her spiritual government among them. But we have also seen the efforts of the emperors to dominate the Church and to make it the instrument of their political ambitions and passion for power. Formerly there was but one emperor to deal with. We shall now see a succession of inde-

[2] Not until Louis Veuillot in France in the mid-nineteenth century, and Chesterton and C. S. Lewis in England in the twentieth, did Christianity regain the initiative in this "war of wits." Perhaps I should add Orwell also, because of *Animal Farm*—though he was hardly a Christian.

pendent monarchs trying to play the same role and to interfere in the affairs of the Church to an intolerable extent while claiming to be faithful children of the Church.

This movement began in France during the reign of Louis XIV. The king claimed the right to nominate the bishops, to permit or forbid the communication of papal decisions and the diffusion of papal documents within his territory, and to enjoy the revenues of all vacant sees. When the popes opposed this, the bishops were incited to draw up a statement of principles aimed at limiting the authority of the popes—the total independence of secular princes, the superiority of the Council over the pope, the respect due to the traditions and customs of the local or national churches, etc. These were to be taught in all seminaries and training houses of religious. Although the pope resisted and, at the end, the king had to give up most of his claims, these ideas about "the rights of the Gallican Church" received wide support. The Church of France, deprived of the stimulus of constant guidance from Rome, was seriously weakened in her fight against unbelief.

It was not only France that gave an example of monarchical absolutism. Almost all the Catholic countries of Europe followed her lead. The Gallican claims were adopted in an exaggerated form in Austria by Joseph II, whose tyrannical control of the activity of the Church in the Austrian Empire brought him more than once to the brink of a complete breach with Rome. His example was followed in Spain, in Venice, in Naples, and Sardinia. The Gallican theories were repeated and disseminated in the German-speaking countries by Febronius (John Nicholas von Hontheim, auxiliary Bishop of Treves). The prince-bishops of Germany adopted those doctrines eagerly and sought to limit papal jurisdiction in a manner which astonishes us today. In the middle years of the eighteenth century, kings and bishops inflicted such humiliations on a weakened papacy that its prestige was never in the course of her long history so low as at that time. When we reflect on this, we are led to ask whether the Catholic kings, beginning from Charles V and Philip II himself in the heyday of the Catholic Revival, down to Louis XV and Charles III of Spain, were less harsh and contemptuous of the Vicars of Christ than the Protestant monarchs who had broken away from the faith altogether.

Even more dangerous to Catholic practice was the growth of Jansenism, which repeated condemnations, and even royal decrees against it, failed to destroy. It may be described as a Catholic version of Calvinism, based on the conviction of the total corruption of human nature by the Fall, and the incapacity of the human will to do any good without a grace which, to be genuine, must be irresistible. Hence man's salvation depends entirely on predestination by God. Those predestined to eternal damnation serve, according to this system, to demonstrate God's "justice." If such is the economy of salvation, then the devotions and exercises of piety so prevalent in Catholic countries were useless as means of gaining merit. In particular, the Jansenists set their minds against devotion to the Eucharist and frequent communion. For them, confession and communion were not means of purification and progress but rewards to those justified by the grace of God.

The Jansenists were also implacable adversaries of the devotion to the Sacred Heart. The Jesuits, who propagated this devotion, encouraged frequent communion, and took pains to safeguard in their theological teaching the free cooperation of man with grace, were the objects of the special hatred of the Jansenists who, for that matter, detested religious orders in general. In their theories of grace the Jansenists appealed to the doctrines of St. Augustine in his writings against the Pelagians. The original "text" of the school was the "Augustinus" of Jansenius, a Dutch theologian. But the great champions of Jansenism in France were St. Cyran, the two Arnaulds, the

Benedictine nuns of Port Royal ("pure as angels, proud as devils") and later, Quesnel. Their writings, their subterfuges, and the protection given to them by many bishops gave a great vogue to their teaching and slowly drained the very sap of Catholic life in France.

The Deists and the unbelievers who had vowed the destruction of the Church, *écraser l'infâme*, saw that, within her ranks, weakened though they were by Gallicanism, Jansenism, and other disturbing developments such as the false mysticism of the Quietists, there was one body of men who stuck to the defence of the Church with a literary skill and doctrinal competence which the philosophers could not laugh away. These were men of perfect orthodoxy of belief and unswerving loyalty to the Holy See, the Society of Jesus. In them the spirit of the Catholic Revival was still incarnate. All the forces of the anti-Catholic world were therefore concentrated on achieving their destruction, and in this the Gallicans and Jansenists became their willing allies. The story of that conspiracy, the obstinate, ruthless campaign in one country after another, the incredible combination of deceit, treachery, and cupidity, may be read in the pages of any reputable history of the Church.

The first country which gave the example was Portugal, where the utterly unscrupulous minister, the Marquis of Pombal, succeeded in convincing a decadent and immoral prince that the Jesuits were his chief adversaries. The society was suppressed by royal decree in all Portuguese territories, all their possessions were confiscated, and the members either thrown into prison or sent into exile. The countries under the rule of the Bourbon princes soon followed, and the unbelievers greeted each successive step with exultation. France came next. The excuse and starting point was a financial disaster in Martinique, a French colony, in which the Jesuit mission was involved. It led to a legal process during which the enemies of the Society were reinforced by the Marquise de Pompadour, the mistress of Louis XV. They then combined with the Parliament of Paris and many provincial parliaments—always enemies of the Society—to demand its suppression as an organization of criminals. Louis XV, a weak and immoral character, knew that the charges were false. Still, he thought that he had to yield in order to be left in peace. So, in spite of the protests of Pope Clement XIII, and of the bishops and clergy of France, he signed the decree of suppression within the territory of France.

It was in Spain that the Society, Spanish in its origin, was most firmly established, with schools, colleges, and residences which had become an essential part of the Catholic life of the country. Moreover, the king of Spain, Charles III, was considered a devout and loyal Catholic. To win him over, his minister had a harder task than Pombal in Portugal or Choiseul in France. It is said that the king was told that the Jesuit confessor of his mother had spread the rumour that he was an illegitimate son. Whatever the mysterious reason for the change of attitude of the king, from a certain moment he became the most implacable adversary of the Society among all the monarchs of Europe. Secret "inquiries" were made and reports about the machinations and immorality of the Jesuits were presented to the king, but never shown to anyone else. In 1767 he signed the decree by which all the Jesuits in the Spanish Empire were arrested and, in conditions of utter misery, put on board sailing vessels and sent to the Papal States. The energetic defender of the Jesuits, Pope Clement XIII, is said to have cried, addressing Charles III, "And you too, my son?"

Two other princes of the Spanish royal house, the King of Naples and the Duke of Parma, followed the example of Spain and suppressed the order in their territories. Of the 23,000 Jesuits who made up the Society before the suppression, the decrees of Portugal, Spain, France, Naples, and Parma had affected more than half. The remainder were mainly in the Austrian Empire, in the Italian states, and in mission territories. Even Maria Theresa of Austria became lukewarm in her support of them. Seeing this, the governments of France, Spain, and Naples demanded of Clement XIII the suppression of the Society in the entire Church. Clement indignantly refused and once again paid a supreme tribute to the Society and its achievements, approving its institute and confirming its privileges. Worn out by these struggles, he died in 1769.

The conclave that gathered at this fateful moment selected Lorenzo Ganganelli, a Franciscan, who also chose the name of Clement. He had not the energy and firmness of Clement XIII. He tried to gain time and to placate the enemies by an attitude of severity towards the Jesuits, removing them from every office of importance and refusing to admit them into his presence. But this did not avail. The enemies would be content with nothing less than death. In July 1773, by the brief *Dominus ac Redemptor,* Clement XIV, without admitting any of the accusations against the Society and dwelling only on the strife and opposition which they had stirred up, decreed the suppression of the order throughout the Church.

The Jesuits had been among the chief architects of the Catholic Revival. That Revival included not only the reform and extension of the Church, which the Council of Trent inaugurated and fostered, but also the strengthening of the Catholic monarchies of Europe on a firm and prosperous basis. This had been secured by halting the Protestant advance and by defeating the Turks at Lepanto. Among these monarchies, Poland had an honoured place. It was a great bastion in the defence of Catholic Christendom against Protestant, Orthodox, and Turkish enemies. Now, about the time of the suppression of the Society, the leading powers of Europe joined together to perpetrate one of the greatest crimes of European history, the suppression of the independence of Poland and its dismemberment and division among Protestant Prussia, Orthodox Russia, and Catholic Austria.

Shortly thereafter, the storm of the French Revolution burst on Europe. The absolute monarchies were swept away one after another. At first the Church suffered as much as the kings. France, "eldest daughter of the Church," did what the reformers had failed to do: the faith itself was proscribed, and the Goddess of Reason enthroned on the altar of Notre Dame. The condition of the Church was once again not unlike what it had been on the eve of the Tridentine Reform. The wheel had come full circle.

There is a final item to be noted in this story of regression and decay, the fortunes of the Church in the missionary world. From the account of the experiments made by Ricci and De Nobili and the open door which they left to their successors in the great civilizations of the East, one would have expected that the movement of conversion would have gone on apace and that the Church would have added to her cultural heritage more and more of the riches of these ancient civilizations. And indeed, for nearly a hundred years after the death of the pioneers, the Jesuit missionaries in China and India gained ground and brought into the Church large numbers of the middle and upper classes. Catholic participation in the promotion of literature and science in China became an accepted fact, and the Christian faith was no longer considered alien and professed only by "barbarians." Under Schall and Verbiest, the Jesuit court astronomers became men of the highest importance and trusted counsellors of the emperor. It did not seem impossible that through the influence of the emperors, perhaps the conversion of one or other of them—there were already converts in the imperial family—the entire Celestial Empire might be gained over to Catholicism.

In India the odds had been even greater against success because of the profoundly religious character of Hindu civilization. The attachment of the people to their religious observances was much greater than in China. But missionaries of the school of De Nobili succeeded in using the very multiplicity of sects and religious groups to the advantage of the Church. They represented Catholicism as one of the authentic *margas*, or ways of salvation, and as one which was in many ways superior to the accepted *margas* of Hinduism.[3] They could show the similarity of Christian teaching and religious sentiment with the purest of Hindu religious schools, that of *bhakti*, or tender devotion to a God of love and grace. The susceptibilities of the Hindus in social and caste questions were respected. They were permitted forms of worship—language, external gestures, ceremonials—which were not alien and emotionally disturbing. The literary achievements of some of the missionaries in the Indian languages were astonishing, and made the Hindus feel that these scholars were men of their own culture. In this respect, two great names deserve to be mentioned. Even before the founding of the Madura Mission and the inauguration of the methods of De Nobili, one of the first Englishmen to come to India, the Jesuit Thomas Stephens, had mastered the Konkani-Marathi tongue to such a degree that his *purana*, or epic poem, on the creation and redemption is considered to be one of the classics of the Marathi language. A century later Joseph Beschi, an Italian like De Nobili and one of the great figures of Tamil literature, wrote the *Tembavani*, an epic poem on St. Joseph, which is also a classic of that difficult language and style of poetry. Beschi, known as Veeramamuniver, "the noble ascetic," is also one of the pioneers of Tamil prose, and the writer of one of the first systematic grammars of the Tamil language.

[3] For example, *jnana marga*, salvation through knowledge or inner "illumination"; *karma marga*, through good works, mainly duties of state; *bhakti marga*, through devotion to a personal God.

But all these great beginnings and fair promises in China and India were destined to be arrested and ended, once again because of internal opposition and misunderstanding. The so-called Chinese and Malabar rites—the honour given to the dead, and particularly the omission of the *epphetha* ceremony in baptism—were denounced to Rome by missionaries of other religious orders who considered the Jesuits to be dangerous innovators and even heretics. The national pride and exclusiveness of the European nations resented the honour given to alien cultures. They could not appreciate a method which prevented the diffusion of their own cultures. Moreover, the growing opposition to the Jesuit Order in Europe, and the presence of powerful adversaries in positions of importance even in Rome, strengthened the hands of those who opposed the method of "adaptation." In response to their demands the pope sent out an inspector, Cardinal de Tournon, to report on the actual working of the system in China and in India. His inquiry was made in the most perfunctory manner, the Chinese and Malabar rites were condemned, and the Jesuits were ordered to give up as rapidly as possible some of the innovations they had introduced.

The result of the decree in China was disastrous. The emperor turned immediately against the missionaries who followed the directives of Rome and in a short time the entire movement of conversions to the Church was arrested. In India the immediate effect was not so disastrous, but the stream of conversions of people of caste thinned and died away. The Church tended to become, outside the Oriental group of Malabar, once again the Church of the Feringhees and the lower castes. A few years later came the suppression of the Society, and this completed the destruction of most of their once prosperous missions. Many of the Christians were left without pastors because other missionaries did not come in sufficient numbers to take the place of the departed Jesuits. Some of the converts reverted to Hinduism. Others went over to Protestantism, which had now been made active as a missionary agency. A great experiment had ended in disappointment and apparent failure. Let us conclude by quoting Arnold Toynbee's weighty judgement on this experiment. It ends on a note of hope which will relieve the sombreness of the picture which I have sketched in the foregoing pages:

In China and India, the Jesuits did not make the mistakes which they had made in Japan of letting their preaching of Christianity fall under the suspicion of being conducted in the political interests of aggressive Western Powers. The Jesuits' approach to their enterprise of propagating Christianity in China was so different and so promising in itself, and it is so much to the point today, that our discussion of the Asian peoples' encounter with the West would be incomplete if we did not take into consideration the line which the Jesuits in India and China opened out. Instead of trying, as we have been trying since their day, to disengage a secular version of Western Civilization from Christianity, the Jesuits tried to disengage Christianity from the non-Christian ingredients in the Western Civilization, and to present Christianity to the Hindus and the Chinese not as the local religion of the West, but as a universal religion with a message for all mankind. The Jesuits stripped Christianity of its accidental and irrelevant Western accessories, and offered the essence of it to China in a Chinese and to India in a Hindu intellectual and literary dress in which there was no incongruous Western embroidery to jar on Asian sensibilities. This experiment miscarried at the first attempt through the faults of domestic feuds within the bosom of the Roman Catholic Church of the day which had nothing to do with Christianity or China or India; but considering that Christianity and China and India are still on the map, we may expect—and hope—to see the experiment tried again.[4]

[4] *The World and the West,* pp. 63–64.

CHAPTER VII

THE CATHOLIC RESTORATION
—PHASE I

As reformation in the sixteenth, so revolution in the eighteenth century, brought death and destruction to the Church in many ways: priests and religious were deported and martyred by the thousands, churches closed down, schools, colleges, and universities taken over by the secular government, religious orders suppressed. What France had done in the eighteenth century, many other countries did in the nineteenth by the revolutions of 1848. The Photian Schism had separated the Eastern Church from Rome. The Protestant Reformation had detached most of the northern nations from Catholic unity. The Revolution, however, was a phenomenon of the Catholic and Latin countries. Thus, even more than at the epoch of the Reformation, the end of the Church seemed near; the aim of the philosophers to "crush the infamous one," *écraser l'infâme*, seemed to be on the verge of fulfilment.

But the Church, "so often doomed, but destined not to die,"[1] was to rise again from the ashes with renewed vigour, to demonstrate to those who had looked on "the scandal of the Church" the more striking "miracle of the Church." The Catholic Restoration, which began in the nineteenth century, has had its ups and downs. But it was a restoration the energies of which have not abated, and with implications which have

[1] Dryden in "The Hind and the Panther." This brilliant allegory was Dryden's defence of the Church after his conversion.

not yet been worked out. The post-conciliar Church of today, which is carrying out a work of reform and readjustment, is continuing the Restoration which began in the Napoleonic period. We shall study this long period in two phases, the first covering the nineteenth century and the twentieth till the end of World War I, and the second phase from Pius XI to our own day. Then, in a subsequent chapter we shall make a survey of the missionary Church during the same period.

The external conditions which favoured the resurgence of Catholicism were, to some extent, the results of the very spirit of the Revolution and a consequence of its success, for the Revolution swept away the absolute monarchies which had humiliated the popes and reduced the Church to helplessness in the previous century. It is true that the Napoleonic settlement brought back the rulers, but their absolute claims were tempered by concessions to popular sentiment. The rise of democracy brought relief and the beginnings of real liberty to the Church. This liberalism, however, was vitiated by an anti-Catholic attitude on many points and by an unacceptable ideal of unmixed secularism which led to continuous clashes between the Church and the new liberal states. Of this we shall speak more fully later on.

Here let us note the fruits of the peace which Napoleon gave to the Church with the Concordat of 1801. This is one of the crucial dates in the history of Catholicism and one that had a profound effect on the social thinking of the Church and the evolution of relations between church and state, between the spiritual and the temporal powers. All this has a direct bearing on the question that occupies us, namely the Church's attitude to man's secular activity, to his social and cultural achievements—in a word, to civilization. France, in the Napoleonic concordat, by negotiating with the pope and by restoring conditions of relative liberty to the Church, disowned by that very fact some of the Gallican pretensions. This French concordat became the model for similar agreements with the constitutional monarchies of many other countries of Europe. Under the guarantees which they gave to the Church, there began a movement of Catholic restoration which developed and spread over the whole of Europe.[2] Let us note some of the features of that restoration.

The concordats regulated the question of the number and the limits of the dioceses in each country, while the popes retained the power of nominating the bishops subject to the consent of the rulers. The churches, seminaries, and monasteries were returned to the Church and the training of a competent secular clergy was once again taken in hand by the bishops. There was also a restoration of religious orders. The Benedictines and the Dominicans came back to active life and ever-increasing influence. The Society of Jesus was restored by Pope Pius VII and soon resumed its vast work of education and of reviving spiritual life by missions and retreats. At the same time a large number of new religious congregations, chiefly of women, began working for the education of women on a massive scale. Thus, even though the universities were secularized and the liberal governments tended to take primary and secondary education into their hands, the Church fought for and retained the right to set up her own schools. These private schools, conducted in large measure by the religious orders, were powerful instruments of the Catholic Restoration.

The great literary movement known as the Romantic Revival also played an important part in exciting interest in Catholicism. It gave to the readers of the new and rich literature, which Romanticism inspired, a new respect for Catholicism.

---

[2] The magnanimous Pius VII never forgot this, even though Napoleon later heaped all kinds of indignities on him. After Waterloo, he welcomed to papal Rome Napoleon's disinherited family and gave them the security which they could not have found elsewhere.

It gave fascinating pictures of the Middle Ages, of conditions of life under feudalism, and of the age of chivalry in which Catholicism was the supreme spiritual force. Newman has recalled in the *Apologia* the influence of Sir Walter Scott and of Coleridge and other writers of the English Romantic school in familiarizing English Protestant readers with Catholic life in the Middle Ages. This literary movement had its counterpart in art through the Gothic Revival and later on through the pre-Raphaelite school of painting and the art criticism of Ruskin. All this was in refreshing contrast to the arid rationalism of the eighteenth century, which had fostered the unbelief of the French philosophers.

The sympathetic knowledge of the many aspects of medieval life enlarged the vision of nineteenth-century man and gave him some idea of the range and riches of Catholic culture. Obviously this could not but aid the religious Restoration. Chateaubriand, one of the leaders of French Romanticism, gave eloquent expression to what may be called the literary, or poetic, approach to Catholicism in his famous *Genius of Christianity*. The volumes of Don Prosper Gueranger, the restorer of the Benedictine Order in France, on the liturgy and the liturgical year, added another important element to the understanding of medieval life and to the devotional aspect of the Catholic Restoration. It is enough here to note the beginnings of the liturgical revival, which was destined to have such wide diffusion and to receive its crown and fulfilment in our own day.

No account of the nineteenth-century revival of Catholicism can be complete without a mention of the Oxford Movement and the significance of the personality and writings of John Henry Newman. Newman took his disciples and readers back, not to the Church of the Middle Ages, but to the Patristic Church and to the theological writings of the great fathers of the Eastern and Western Church. His own affinities were not with the thinkers of the Scholastic period but with the mind and spirit of the patristic age. His greatest service to the Church was the proof of theological continuity in the history of the Church, the demonstration that the Catholic Church of his day had all the essential features of the primitive Church and the Church of the fathers. (See *The Development of Christian Doctrine,* Newman's major contribution to the theological thinking of the Church.) By this means he destroyed the Protestant hypothesis of the doctrinal corruption of the Church and the divine mission of the reformers to return to primitive Christian practice. He was also a brilliant controversialist and one of the great preachers of modern times. The exquisite beauty of his style and the intense human interest of the *Apologia* give him an assured place in English literature. His personal holiness has led to his cause of beatification being introduced before the Holy See. The scope and stature of the man have been compared to those of the great fathers of the Church. It is certain that he has affected more than any other single person the fortunes of Western Christendom in modern times.[3]

I should also mention here a remarkable testimony to the vitality of the Church and to the inner force which enabled her to recover from the repeated crises which threatened her existence in the course of her long history. I refer to Macaulay's famous essay written in 1840 on Ranke's *History of the Popes.* After recounting some of the vicissitudes of her history, Macaulay concludes with the well-known passage:

> The history of that Church joins together the two great ages of human civilization. No other institution is left standing which carries the mind back to the time when

[3] A critic of literature, George Sampson, has spoken of him as "this man with the head of a Caesar, the pen and tongue of a Cicero, and the heart and fervour of a St. Philip Neri."

the smoke of sacrifice rose from the Pantheon and when cameleopards and tigers bounded in the Flavian amphi-theatre. The proudest royal houses are but of yesterday when compared with the line of the Supreme Pontiffs. That line we trace back in an unbroken series from the pope who crowned Napoleon in the 19th century to the pope who crowned Pepin in the 8th; and far beyond the time of Pepin the august dynasty extends, till it is lost in the twilight of fable. The republic of Venice came next in antiquity. But the republic of Venice was modern when compared to the Papacy; and the republic of Venice is gone, and the Papacy remains. The Papacy remains not in decay, not a mere antique, but full of life and youthful vigour.

The Catholic Church is still sending forth to the far-thest ends of the world missionaries as zealous as those who landed in Kent with Augustine and still confronting hostile kings with the same spirit with which she con-fronted Attila. The number of her children is greater than in any former age. Her acquisitions in the New World have more than compensated her for what she has lost in the Old. Her spiritual ascendancy extends over the vast countries which lie between the plains of the Missouri and Cape Horn, countries which a century hence may not improbably contain a population as large as that which now inhabits Europe. The members of her communion are certainly not fewer than a hundred and fifty millions;[4] and it will be difficult to show that all other Christian sects united amount to a hundred and twenty millions.

Nor do we see any sign which indicates that the term of her long dominion is approaching. She saw the com-mencement of all the governments and all the ecclesiasti-

[4] It is over five hundred million today.

cal establishments that now exist in the world; and we feel no assurance that she is not destined to see the end of them all. She was great and respected before the Saxon had set foot on Britain, before the Frank had passed the Rhine, when Grecian eloquence still flourished in Antioch, when idols were still worshipped in the temple of Mecca. And she may still exist in undiminished vigour when some traveller from New Zealand shall, in the midst of a vast solitude, take his stand on a broken arch of London Bridge to sketch the ruins of St. Paul's.

Macaulay has the reputation of being a brilliant but superficial writer. In this essay, however, as Frederick Harrison remarked, he perceived a truth which the current Protestant prejudices prevented others from seeing and gave it resounding expression. This was an example of quite unusual penetration. His words constitute a proof of what the fathers of the First Vatican Council later said, namely, that the history and activity of the Church constitute an apologetic argument of great force, the *signum levatum in coelis,* a banner raised aloft in the skies.

There are two other examples of the same vitality of the Church and of her supernatural power to renew the faith and fervour of her people which should be mentioned here. First are the apparitions of Lourdes and the immense movement of world-wide pilgrimages which it created and which continue to this day. The miracles of Lourdes, and the greater, continuing miracle of the faith and patience of the endless stream of sufferers and pilgrims who fill that hallowed spot with the murmur of their prayers and the exultant strains of their hymns, has been a source of spiritual energy for the Church. The second is the life of the curé of Ars, and the crowds that went to Ars to confess to him and hear his words. This was the living example of God's use of the poor and despised things of

the earth to confound the wise and the strong, and as a model
for parish priests all over the world, stirring them up to
achieve both spiritual perfection in their own lives and an ardent zeal for souls of others.

The history of Catholicism in the nineteenth century, however, was not one of uninterrupted progress and success. There
were still many formidable obstacles to be overcome so that
the Church might carry out her spiritual mission and her role
of guide in those aspects of secular activity which are connected with the spiritual destiny of man. The earliest of these
obstacles came from the yet unsolved question of the precise
nature of the relations between church and state. Uncertainty
still reigned within the Church and outside regarding the
limits of each one's competence. The monarchs who regained
their thrones after the storm of the Revolution had many of
the old absolutist pretensions and Napoleon himself tried to
exercise some of the prerogatives which the Gallican monarchs had claimed. His early friendly relations with the
Church and the papacy were afterwards darkened by his an-
nexation of the Papal States and by the captivity of Pope
Pius VII.

After Napoleon's downfall, the democratic movement in
Europe developed along lines which the Church could not
entirely approve, although basically the Church had no opposition to the idea of political liberty and representative government.[5] As we shall see, the extension of representative

[5] (See Chapter V for Catholic upholders of the sovereignty of the
people.)
While the Church had no objection to democracy, it could not
approve Rousseau's principle of the absolute value of the *vol-
onté générale* and the implied indifference to the rights of the
person if he happened to be in the minority. Neither could it approve the *laissez-faire* of liberal economics and its indifference to

government actually helped the Church in many ways. But the concrete manifestation of democracy in Europe, in the form of the liberal state, included the formulation of a body of doctrine—political, social, and economic,—which the Church lost little time in disapproving. The state declared itself completely independent of the Church and of the spiritual power, refused all cooperation and help to it, and fostered a "secularism" which was essentially godless. It is in the context of this religious indifferentism and practical atheism that we must understand the condemnation of De Lammenais and the French "liberal" Catholics who wished the Church to come to terms with the liberal state. The same reasons explain the condemnation of the propositions contained in the *Syllabus* of Pius IX.

Along with the growth of a secularist, anti-clerical liberalism, there was also an extraordinary development of nationalism. In Italy the combined forces of the two movements led to the overrunning of the Papal States and the creation of united Italy. The maintenance of the political authority of the popes over the papal provinces had become very difficult owing to the inefficiency of the papal government and the opposition to it of large sections of the people. The ill advised readiness of the pope to retain his temporal power with the help of Austrian and French troops did not facilitate a peaceful settlement with the Italian people. When the French troops were withdrawn in 1870, as a consequence of the Franco-Prussian War, the Italian nationalists occupied what remained of the Papal States. The pope could not possibly acquiesce in any settlement which would make him the subject of a temporal sovereign, and so he protested against his forcible dispossession of his territory and assumed the posture of the "Prisoner

---

the rights of society and to the concept of the "common good." Later events, political and economical, were to justify abundantly the stand taken by the Church.

of the Vatican." For a satisfactory solution of this question the papacy had to wait sixty years.

The liberal dream of destroying the power and prestige of the papacy and reducing the Church to a position of total dependence on secular power was doomed to be completely shattered. The diminution of the temporal power and its final eradication brought about an extraordinary increase in the moral authority of the papacy. The personalities of the popes from Pius IX onwards evoked the love and admiration of all Catholics. In the doctrinal sphere, the convoking of the First Vatican Council—which was the largest gathering of Bishops which the Church had ever seen—and the definition of papal infallibility, destroyed the last vestiges of Gallican thought that might have lingered within the Church. The government of the Church became organized and centralized under the pope and his curia to a degree never known before. It was to be embodied in the new *Code of Canon Law* which was promulgated by Benedict XV in 1921. That event may be said to mark the end of the first phase of the Catholic Restoration. But before we reach that point, we must note certain developments of the highest interest to our theme.

The pope who succeeded Pius IX was one of the leading statesmen of the nineteenth century and one of the greatest of all popes, Leo XIII. He had been out of sympathy with the political intransigence of Pius IX's later years, and he wished to come to terms with the best elements of the contemporary world so as to secure for the Church the influence which might enable her to counteract the dangerous and unchristian currents in that world. He realized that, though Catholicism had a historical attachment to monarchy and an ideological sympathy with it, there was not only no opposition between Catholicism and democracy, but there were many features of Catholic life and doctrine which fostered democratic instincts. Moreover, in the sixteenth century, against the teaching of the

theorists of absolutism and the "divine right of kings," the great
Catholic thinkers and theologians—e.g., Bellarmine and Vázquez—had developed the doctrine of the sovereignty of the
people, although they had exposed it differently from Rousseau, for whom the consent of the people created the power
which the ruler was to exercise. According to Rousseau, the
power of the state came from the accumulation of individual
rights which were freely handed over to the ruler by the ruled.
This involved a pragmatic concept of morality and the possibility, even the certainty, of majority tyranny over a minority
and of indifference to the rights of the individual as a human
person. We shall see that the "liberal" democrats were to be-
tray their cause and the liberties of the people they ruled, in
a terrible manner at a later period.

Leo XIII and the Catholic political thinkers were quite willing to admit and approve the democratic or parliamentary
form of government insofar as it was consistent with the
Catholic concept of the common good and the natural law.
They asserted that it was God who granted to the state the
power which it exercised. Moreover, the sharing of political
power by the masses gave to the Catholic populations a political influence which enabled the Church to defeat the efforts of
absolute rulers to enslave her. This was triumphantly shown
by the struggle of the Catholic Centre under Windthorst
against Bismarck's *Kulturkampf,* a struggle in which Bismarck
was compelled eventually to capitulate and to make the most
notable modern repetition of the journey to Canossa.

The most farsighted example of Pope Leo's effort to come
to terms with modern governments and to exercise a legitimate spiritual influence over them was his appeal to the
Catholics of France to make peace with the republic and
thereby to secure in the government of their country the part
and voice which their numbers could ensure to them. But this
proposal did not enjoy the adhesion which political wisdom

should have dictated. The monarchist elements remained sullenly aloof, and the bishops and religious orders stood with them to a large extent. The republic became more and more anti-clerical. Later on the famous Dreyfus affair complicated the situation still more and sharpened all the old antipathies. This led ultimately to the disestablishment of the Church in France and to the growth of "laicisation" and of the sectarian secularist state which was to do much harm to the Church in Europe.

There was another aspect of democracy, or liberalism, which also claimed the attention of that great pope in a way that was to leave a lasting impression on the policy of the Church. Liberal economics had led to the growth of capitalism and all the social injustice involved in the policy of economic *laissez-faire* and ruthless competition. The rich were becoming richer and the poor poorer, creating by degrees the proletariat class, which lived in conditions akin to slavery. This was true of the individual workers and, under the colonial system with its economic exploitation of the subject nations, it was coming to be true of entire countries. The consequence of all this had been the development of socialism and the revolutionary theories of Karl Marx. While the most successful forms of capitalism had developed in the Protestant countries—in England and Germany, and later on in the United States—the industrialists in Catholic countries were also swimming with the current. The apostasy of the working classes and the preparation for the Communist domination of later years was being effectively prepared.

Leo XIII perceived the danger, and even before him the German Catholic Congress at Mainz had turned its attention to the evil. In Germany's Bishop Ketteler the Catholic social movement had found a great leader whose example, unfortunately, was not followed by many. But Leo XIII, in his encyclical *Rerum novarum,* analyzed the situation, or condition, of the workers with masterly understanding and knowledge. He outlined the rights of the worker to a decent living standard for himself and his family and to the right to exercise his liberty in social and political matters. All this was, of course, within the framework of Christian faith and the primacy of the spiritual; it was the Catholic answer to materialistic socialism. And *Rerum novarum* remains one of the great documents of Catholicism, a milestone in the Church's intervention in the secular activity of man.

Unfortunately Leo XIII's appeal to the Catholic industrialists and Catholic governments had only a partial success. The full effects of the initiatives of the great pope were to appear later on, during the second phase of the Restoration. On the one hand, the secular states, dominated by the passion for nationalism and imperialism, went on in their proud, unheeding way, paying scant attention to Christian ideals—a course of action which was to involve them in the terrible catastrophe of World War I. In the meantime the socialist movement was also gaining strength. Large sections of the workers in Catholic and Protestant countries had adopted the Marxist solution and had enrolled themselves in the ranks of atheistic communism. They had accepted the thesis that religion was the "opium of the masses." The Russian Revolution coincided with the closing stages of the world conflict. Russia had made a separate peace with Germany by the Treaty of Brest-Litovsk, and then set up her Communist regime. When the main conflict ended and the Treaty of Versailles was signed, the Church found herself impoverished and weakened.

In Russia, there began a ruthless campaign of political expansion and atheistic propaganda that was to tear away from the Church millions of her children in eastern Europe. In the West, the Catholic Austro-Hungarian Empire was dismembered. Most of the Catholic population of the western countries lay torn and bleeding from the cruel wounds of war. The

Protestant powers—England, the United States, and even Germany—emerged stronger than before. The liberal anti-clerical element in these democratic countries ensured that the papacy should be excluded from the discussions of Versailles.[6] In spite of the magnificent work of Leo XIII—his adjustment to the new social and political conditions of Europe, his incentives to biblical and philosophical studies, his efforts to revitalize spiritual life, and his success in raising the moral prestige of the papacy—the Church on the morrow of World War I found herself isolated and obliged to assume a defensive attitude.

It took the horrors of another world conflict—the events that led to it and followed it—and the courage and wisdom of three remarkable popes to break that isolation and to launch the Church on the many-sided action on a world-wide scale which we witness today. We shall study these developments in the following chapters.

[6] I refer to the "secret clause" in the preparatory Treaty of London, whereby the Allies agreed that the Vatican not be invited to participate in the peace conference. It was due mainly to Sonnino, the Italian delegate, who dreaded a possible discussion of the Roman Question. The same anti-clerical bias caused the cold reception given to the farsighted "Peace Proposals" of Benedict XV, which, if heeded, might have prevented the twenty years' tension which preceded World War II.

CHAPTER VIII

THE CATHOLIC RESTORATION
—PHASE II

Our glance at the pontificate of Leo XIII and the nature of his farsighted efforts to adapt the Church to the changing social conditions of his time constituted what we are now accustomed to call an *aggiornamento,* a bringing up to date of the Church. In reality, as we have seen repeatedly in the foregoing pages, the Church has always fostered the spirit of *aggiornamento,* because she has always recognized the need for a continuing reform of herself. Obviously, the necessity for such reform became more urgent, and the process of adaptation more manifest, at certain crucial epochs of her history than at others. This was because the movement of change in the external forms of civilization was more pronounced, more "revolutionary," at certain well-known periods.

Let us, however, recall once more the basic fact that, while the Church adapted herself to the changing conditions around her, she did not add anything substantially new to her inheritance of revealed truth; rather, she helped the external forms of social and cultural living to enrich themselves in the light of those essential and indispensable truths. The adaptations of the Church certainly imply a process of give and take; but from the point of view of ultimate values, the giving was more important than the taking. In the manner of the great apostle, the Church makes herself "all things to all men" in order to gain all.

Though, as I said, there have been several earlier examples

of reform and readjustment, it is only fair to say that, in the *aggiornamento* of Pope John XXIII and the Council which he summoned, and in all the constructive work it has done and is doing, there are certain features which make that term peculiarly applicable to the present phase of Catholic reform. The Catholic reconstruction of the Tridentine period was, to a large extent, a defensive movement; it concerned itself chiefly with the condemnation of the many destructive heresies. There was a negative side even to the positive reform which it introduced. The insistence on many points of Catholic faith and practice was very emphatic—even, so far as practical consequences are concerned, overemphatic—because of the Protestant denials of those points. Such was the case with the use of Latin as the language of the liturgy and as a means of communication, the invocations to the saints and the encouragement of devotion to them, the insistence on tradition and the teaching authority of the Church as a criterion of truth (against the Protestants' exclusive reliance on the Bible), the concept of the Church as a visible juridical body as against the theory of a purely spiritual Church, and so on.

At the Council of Trent, Catholic doctrine was affirmed as much by anathema and condemnation as by positive enunciation. This tradition continued in the Church, and is seen in the repeated condemnations of errors in the nineteenth century, especially by Pius IX; in some of the decrees of the Vatican Council I; and in the condemnation of modernism by Pius X. Vatican II, under Pope John's guidance, was singularly free from such negative methods. John is said to have counted the "condemnations" in the first draft of a certain theological decree and thrown up his hands in impatience. The almost wholly constructive approach of Vatican II is a striking characteristic of our latest *aggiornamento*.

Before we come to John XXIII and Vatican II, we should glance at the constructive work of Pius XI and of Pius XII,

both of whom belong decisively to this phase. Pius XI brought
to the papacy something of the fresh breath of the mountains
he loved so well. He had the courage to settle the Roman
Question by a formula which seems to be a living symbol of
the relationship between church and state—a relationship
which, at last, after so many fluctuations and uncertainties,
seems to be moving towards its final and definitive formulation.
The Church claimed and secured in this settlement complete
independence from the secular power. The pope became temporal sovereign of a little slip of territory of not more than a
few square acres. That sovereignty, however, ensures for him
total freedom of action and facility of relations with the rest of
the world and precludes his becoming involved in the problems
of temporal government and the ambiguities of political action
which have done so much harm to the Church in the past. From
this position of independence, the Church can negotiate with
all temporal powers for the solution of those mixed questions
in which church and state have concurrent jurisdiction[1]—questions of the education of youth, the recognition of Christian
marriage, the right of organization of Catholics in the pursuit of
religious objectives, the freedom of private and public worship,
the right to oppose legislation involving obligations on Catholic
citizens which might go against their consciences. The Concordat with the Italian Government, which was signed at the
same time as the Lateran Treaty on the Roman Question, was
considered a model of such agreements between church and
state.

Whatever we may think of the political system which Mussolini tried to establish in Italy, we can join Pope Pius XI in
praising him for that freedom from the old liberal anti-clerical-

------

[1] I am using here a term peculiar to political science which desig-
nates a jurisdiction common to the central and state governments
in a federal structure.

ism which would have made impossible such a settlement as the Lateran Treaty. This appreciation of the role of Mussolini did not prevent the pope from opposing him later with all his might or from using the independence he had gained to proclaim that opposition to the entire world—as happened, for example, when fascism clashed with the Catholic Action organization which was very dear to Pope Pius XI. It was one of his most significant contributions to the Phase II of the Restoration because it marked the beginnings of that active encouragement of the lay apostolate which was to be developed still more by Pius XII and was to find its fullest expression in Vatican II.

That clash with Mussolini was but one incident in the struggle against the totalitarian state of which we do not yet see the end. It is a far more deadly struggle than those with the liberal state or with the empire. The persecutions which it has brought on the Church can be equalled in vehemence only by those launched by the pagan emperors of Rome. The concept of the dignity and freedom of the human person is implicit in the very notion of Christian salvation, as is that of the primacy of the spiritual over the temporal, which the Church taught from the very beginning of her existence. Man is to be saved by an act of faith freely made, and the free acceptance of the obligation which it involves. Faith in Christ and adhesion to him makes him a member of the mystical body of Christ and gives him, as we saw in the opening pages of this book, a participation in the dignity and prerogatives of Christ himself. This vocation to divine sonship through Jesus is a universal vocation to which all men, whatever their race, are called. Thus, the vocation of a Christian postulates and confirms the freedom and the fundamental equality with all men. This was in direct contradiction to the theory and practice of the totalitarian regimes, particularly the Nazi model with its fanatical racial exclusiveness. Hence, the inevitable clash between these regimes and the Church. The last years of Pius XI were troubled by his ever-increasing realization of the danger from those regimes. His warnings and protests were prophetic in their force and vision.

The pontificate of Pius XII was cast in very ominous times. The first years coincided with World War II; after that came the laborious process of political and economic reconstruction in western Europe. Then followed the years of bitter disappointments and frustrations because of the cold war, and the failure of the hopes of disarmament and the impotence to which the United Nations organization was reduced because of it. Pius XII directed the fortunes of the Church in these troubled times with consummate diplomacy and raised the international prestige of the papacy to a height not known before.

During the war, his mediation between the adversaries to alleviate the sufferings of the sick and the imprisoned gained him the deepest respect of all.[2] His role in saving Rome caused him to be acclaimed by a Roman crowd as *Defensor Civitatis* (Defender of the City). When we think of the studied aloofness with which the Italian politicians had treated the popes from Pius IX onwards, and the tension between Pius XI and the Fascist government, we realize the vastness of the change which the action and personality of Pius XII had brought about in the attitude of the Italian people.

But an even more significant change had come over the political circles of the free world in their attitude to the papacy after the emergence of the totalitarian regimes. The opposition to Communist absolutism on the part of the Church did not surprise them—they took that as the expression of religious antagonism. This notwithstanding, they welcomed the "alliance" with the Church against communism, and lips un-

---

[2] We must not forget similar service by Benedict XV during World War I, in conditions less favourable to the Holy See.

accustomed to Christian language even began to mouth phrases like "Christendom" and "Christian civilization." But the unequivocal stand taken by the Church against the brutally repressive autocracy of the Fascist and Nazi regimes, particularly on the issues of the rights of conscience and freedom of the individual, was a revelation to them. They saw that what remained of the liberal democracies in these countries had gone down before the onslaught, but that the Catholic Church—in their minds associated with the "antidemocratic" condemnations of the *Syllabus*—was the last and almost the only defender of human liberty. They were obliged to revise their judgements, for the world saw that it was not the secular inheritors of the revolutionary tradition that were defending the principles of "liberty, equality, and fraternity." Under *their* regimes the exercise of liberty had widened the gulf between rich and poor and suppressed all equality. Those who tried to restore equality, as did the Communists, did away with liberty. Fraternity could never be realized by those who fostered and encouraged colonialism and imperialism and who preached either class warfare or racial discrimination. Those words and the ideal they represented had been put forward in a society which had its ultimate roots in Christian ideas and traditions. Within the framework of Christianity alone could they find a balanced and harmonious realization.

It was clear at that point that those Christian ideals and principles had a validity in the political and economic activity of the contemporary world, and that the total divorce between the Church and public life which the liberals had wished to impose had been fatal even to the best temporal interests of Europe. This realization led to the growth of the Christian Democratic parties in western Europe in the postwar years. They owed much to the initiative of Don Sturzo, who had founded the Italian *Partito Popolare* before the time of Mussolini. The men who formed the new Christian Democratic parties were thoroughly conversant with the social teaching of the Church, and some of them had been trained in the ranks of Catholic Action. They were men inspired by the Catholic vision of universal brotherhood and international harmony, and it is not surprising that the most fervent among them should have been the "founding fathers" of a united Europe. They wanted to construct a positive "new order" capable of resisting communistic ideology and expansionism. That was the role of such men as De Gasperi, Robert Schumann, and Adenauer. Their emergence as European leaders who paid respectful attention to the teaching of the popes and in general to the "magisterium" of the Church added immensely to the prestige of the Church and the authority of the papacy.

Pius XII, with his wide and varied experience as papal Secretary of State, knew well the condition of Europe as it emerged from the storm of war. He exercised, indirectly, beneficial influence on the evolution of the socio-political ideas of the Catholic leaders of Europe. He was a man of the widest intellectual interests in addition to being a profoundly spiritual man. He touched Catholic life at almost every point, speaking with care and authority on subjects almost encyclopedic in their range. He declared his full sympathy with such international organizations as the UN and its affiliated agencies, and he took steps to cooperate with some of them, sending observers to UNESCO and FAO. He met and spoke to groups representing almost every aspect of modern life—to university men, to members of the learned professions, to workers of every category, to artists and to sportsmen. In the sphere of Church reform he initiated great liturgical changes, gave an impetus to biblical studies, and promoted the lay apostolate. Justice has not been done to the depth and amplitude of the achievement of Pope Pius XII. The inevitable reaction after a period of exceptional popularity and the dust of controversy raised about his supposed passivity in the time of Hitler's massacre of the Jews have obscured his figure at the present day. But history will surely vindicate him.

There is, however, no denying the fact that his efforts to break down the isolation of the Church and to secure her rightful place in the manifold activities of contemporary life were handicapped by the reserve and aloofness of his personal manner and by his use of the negative formulas which he had inherited from the past. It required the genial personality, the warm humanity, the immense strength under a deceptively disarming manner of John XXIII to achieve a psychological "breakthrough," as we may call it. We must now turn our attention to him and to the Council with which his name will be forever associated.

It is not easy to sum up the nature and significance of the achievements of Pope John and of the Council to which he gave a particular orientation by his words and tactful guidance. If I were asked to summarize the different features of the combined action and pronouncements of the pope and the Council, I should say that the Church was redefining her attitude to the world and to the activities of the world; she was seeking to enter into those activities in order to give them the quintessence of her own spirit—that "interiority" which would draw them within "the mystery of Christ" and enable them to participate in the Incarnation in its widest implications. In order to achieve this, the Church, remembering that the Lord had condemned not the world in its totality but the worldly spirit, needed to approach the world in a new spirit; not in the spirit of total condemnation, confounding the good with the bad; not even in an attitude of distant approbation as from the seat of judgement; but in an attitude of love, of immediate and "personal" involvement inasmuch as the Church, the mystical body of Christ, represents the person of Christ. The

Church wants to express towards the world the love of the father who "so loved the world that he gave his only begotten Son for its salvation," and the love of the son, of whom every man can say, "He loved me and delivered himself up for me." Pope John radiated this love and gave memorable expression to it in the great encyclicals *Mater et magistra* and *Pacem in terris*. And the Council, because of the vital impulses that are common to popes and to bishops as rulers of the Universal Church, caught the spirit of the pope and reproduced his very accents in their declarations.

Such an attitude to the world, the expression of her true nature and spirit, created a different image of the Church from that which adversaries, or strangers and outsiders, and sometimes even ill-informed children of her own, had of her. In order to be understood and appreciated and accepted in the role of loving mother and wise teacher, it was necessary that she once again, as so often before, turn her glance inward and reflect on herself and tell the world not only what she had always been but also what she intended to be in the rapidly changing and evolving world. Therefore, in all the decrees and declarations of the Council, there is this in common: they are either direct pronouncements on the nature and constitution of the Church, or they are declarations of policy or outlines for future action which throw additional light on that nature and orientation. Hence, we may say that in the Council the Church was engaged mainly in thinking and reflecting about herself; in telling the world about her mission of continuing the work of the Incarnation and Redemption; in describing in what manner that mission impelled her to act with the different categories of men who surrounded her—her own children first, and then those outside her fold. She passionately desired and hoped that the misunderstandings of past centuries might be dissipated, and that her true visage as the bride of

Christ and the mother of all peoples might stand fully revealed.[3]

If we look at the documents which the Council put forth we shall see how true this is. There is first the great dogmatic constitution on the Church, *Lumen gentium;* the decree on the episcopal office, which deals with the "collegiality" of the bishops; the decree on the role and function of the priesthood and on the training of the clergy; decrees on the liturgy, on the missionary apostolate, on the renovation and adaptation of religious life. These documents enshrine in authoritative form the doctrine concerning the Church, its visible and external government and its inner spirit and universal mission.[4]

Next, there are the documents which bear upon the function and position of the "people of God," of the body of Christian people who constitute, along with the teaching Church, the total Church. Those documents are either complete in themselves or are parts of the above-mentioned documents. Thus we have a declaration on the vocation of all men to holiness in the *Lumen gentium;* on the missionary and apostolic duty of all laymen in the document on the missions; there are repeated allusions to the participation by the laity in the liturgical worship of the Church—to their "royal priesthood" as St. Peter calls it—by which they offer the sacrifice of the Mass along with the priest. Lastly there is the important document dealing specifically with the lay apostolate which summarizes the Church's teaching on this subject (a theme which Pius XI and Pius XII had developed in many documents) and gives it a complete, coherent, and solemn formulation.

[3] For a description of the nature and role of the Church, see Introduction.
[4] They will have to be completed by a revision of the Code of Canon Law. A commission has been appointed to undertake this revision.

Before passing on to the other decrees and declarations of the Council, let us indicate the light which this first series of conciliar pronouncements throws on the subject of our particular enquiry—the attitude of the Church to civilizations, her cultural orientation insofar as it results from her spiritual nature and mission. One of the commonest accusations made against her, especially by intellectuals speaking about missionary activity in non-Christian countries, is that she has "identified" herself with western European culture and that in consequence she has given, and according to some *deliberately* given, a political bias to her evangelical work. I have touched on this while speaking of Ricci and De Nobili, and I shall deal with it more in detail in the next chapter. It is enough here to indicate the implications in the contrary sense of two of the documents we have mentioned. First, the declaration on the character and functions of the episcopate and the connected doctrine of "collegiality" brings into the ordinary government of the Church—and this was evident in the extraordinary event of the Council—the participation of a large number of bishops, Africans and Asians, who are not of the Western race and of the Western cultural tradition. Any pro-Western political bias in the government of the Church, even if the prelates of the Western countries wanted to exercise it, will become more and more difficult, not to say impossible.

More radical in its consequences is another decree, that on liturgical reform. The existence of the Oriental Rites in the Church and her consistent efforts to conserve and foster them should be sufficient to refute the allegation of Latin exclusiveness. But the emergence now within the Latin Rite itself, and in the most solemn liturgical actions, of scores of regional or national languages, with their modes of expression and types of music, ends very definitely the predominance of Latin, and the western cultural affinities which Latin undoubtedly created and fostered.

Let us now consider the document on ecumenism and all that it involves. Already in the fourth century, rejecting the express teaching of St. Cyprian, the Church maintained the validity of the baptism conferred by heretics. She thus declared that non-Catholic Christians had in their religious practices authentic channels by which the grace of Christ could reach them and give them basic appurtenance to the mystical body. The validity of the priesthood and the episcopate, and of the Sacraments of the Orthodox and schismatic churches is expressly recognized. It is evident in the very history of these churches that, among their sincere and earnest followers, the spirit of God has worked and brought forth many admirable fruits of charity and holiness. Accurate and unbiased historical research has enabled both sides to understand and appreciate the other in a way that had not been possible in the days when the memories of mutual opposition were still sore, and antipathies were passionate. Moreover, the rise of atheism and of irreligious secularism in the world and in traditionally Christian countries has given to Catholics and to other Christian churches and denominations a common interest to safeguard, and common actions to undertake.

Many Protestants also realized the danger to genuine faith in Christ as Saviour, and in the Scriptures as the word of God, without a divinely instituted authority to define and conserve that faith. There is a nostalgia for unity on both sides, a passionate conviction that Our Lord desired that unity; and an earnest desire to respond to his prayer: *That they may be one.* All this led to touching admissions of faults committed in the past by both sides and declarations that Christians of different sections had much to learn from one another. At the Council, the non-Catholic observers were received with respect and honour and treated as brothers—"Brethren in Jesus Christ," as Pope John called them. The aspirations of some of the followers of the Oxford Movement, the tentative and abortive efforts of such men as Lord Halifax and Cardinal Mercier in regard to Anglicans, seemed now nearer to realization than at any time before. The unfinished work of the Council of Florence on reunion with the Orthodox churches gives every hope of being taken up again with better chances of permanent success. The transformation in the relations between the churches which a few years has brought about is little short of miraculous.

The doctrinal and cultural consequences of all this have been considerable. The Church is promoting biblical studies and scriptural theology, the use of the vernacular tongue in the liturgy, and she is organizing the lay apostolate—unrestrained by the inhibitions and the negative approach on these matters engendered by the Counter Reformation. Moreover, during the centuries of separation from Rome, the Orthodox and the Protestant nations have developed their own type of Christian culture, their schools of religious and secular art, and their own social attitudes. If the ecumenical movement leads at some stage to effective reunion of at least some of these churches, the special achievements of our separated brethren insofar as they are rooted in a common primitive Christian tradition will become part of the Catholic universal heritage. But, even without formal reunion, the close relations now established, the system of common discussions and common social undertakings which are an accepted fact now, will lead to mutual cultural exchanges in increasing proportions.

From the Eastern churches and the Protestants we can learn much in religious art and the expression of religious devotion, in educational and social experiments, in the methods of the missionary apostolate, in the development of civic virtues which are often much more developed among Protestants than among Catholics. The reasons for the backwardness of Catholics in this last point are deep rooted and must be studied in their historical context, but the fact remains that countries of Protestant culture show in general a political stability lacking in very many Catholic countries. The protests of a few groups of "integrists" and "traditionalists" will not halt this movement of mutual exchange.

The ecumenical movement represents the dialogue, described by Pope Paul VI in his encyclical *Ecclesiam suam,* with the separated brethren who form the closest of the circles around the Catholic Church. But working within the same geographical environment, but ideologically much further removed from us and forming another distinct circle, are the followers of a secularist scientific and technological culture. With them, too, the Church wishes to enter into dialogue, and certain documents are addressed more particularly, though not exclusively, to those votaries of an entirely secular culture. They are the protagonists of a humanism which seeks to solve the problems of man's existence and to satisfy his aspirations to happiness and perfection by man's own unaided efforts. They therefore look upon solutions based on belief in God, on the Christian or any other religious system, as being outmoded; mankind in its evolution towards greater perfection has left religion behind it. Such solutions, they assert, might have been useful once, but they are no longer valid. Strongly impressed by the idea of evolution, witnessing the continual flux in the external conditions of man's life, highly critical of anything that cannot be tested and proved by the mathematical and physical sciences, modern man denies the existence of absolute transcendent truth regarding man and his destiny. He believes that he is master of his destiny and can attain the happiness he seeks by the progress of science.

This is no longer the pagan humanism of the sixteenth century which sought man's happiness in the unashamed satisfaction of his human passions and emotions, paying little attention to his moral obligations and supernatural destiny. Against that humanism the Church of the Catholic Revival op-

posed a "devout humanism," bringing into the service of religion all the knowledge of man, of his inner emotions and his
capacities for external actions which the New Learning had
brought. Against the secular materialistic humanism of today,
"the humanism of power" as we may call it, the Church opposes
what we must still call Christian humanism in the widest
sense. We have traced the evolution of the Church's attitude
to the secular activity of Christian believers from the remote
beginnings in the Judaeo-Hellenic world, on through the decisive stages of her history—the Greco-Roman, the Medieval,
the Renaissance, and the modern post-Revolutionary periods.
At each of these stages, in keeping with the widening of man's
social and cultural horizons and the intensification of his activities, the Church enlarged the content of what, for lack of a
better term, I have called her "secular doctrine." The expression may be misleading, however, because the doctrine of the
Church is all of a piece, her secular and spiritual doctrines are
perfectly dovetailed one with the other. "Secular doctrine" has
a wider scope than what is ordinarily known as the "social
doctrine" of the Church because it affects not only the dynam-
ics of social organization but also all the activities—cultural and
scientific—of civilized man in the construction of his "terrestrial city." It has now reached an amplitude which it never had
before; therefore, the impact of the Church on civilizations
both in the non-Christian world and in the paganized circles
of the post-Christian world is wider and stronger than in earlier
ages.

The scientific discoveries of today have helped modern man
to develop a universal outlook and to integrate himself more
fully and more consciously with his material environment. This
responds to the metaphysical vision and theological certainties
of the Church also. Today the Church's secular doctrine, without ever confusing the material and the spiritual, moves towards a synthesis of the social and the physical sciences. There

is, therefore, much common ground, materially speaking, between secular humanism and Christian humanism. In the pronouncements in which these doctrines are exposed, a warm optimism runs through all the references to man's achievements in the material and scientific sphere. The Church understands that not only nature but also the technological environment created by man is capable of raising his mind to the power and greatness of the Creator. Nor does she forget that many of the scientific, technical, and social achievements of modern man, though now divorced from Christian beliefs and employed to undermine the Christian concept of life, have nevertheless Christian roots and in their earlier stages were developed in a Christian society. This fact, and the conviction that even with these aberrations they serve the designs of the Providence of God to bring good out of evil, enables the Church to speak of contemporary man, his greatness and smallness, his triumphs and perplexities, his joys and his anguish, in accents of profound sympathy and maternal love.

We shall find this wide range of doctrine as it stands at present exposed with clarity in the Council's *Constitution on the Church in the Modern World;* in the *Declaration on Religious Liberty;* in the decree on *The Means of Social Communication.* These conciliar documents should be taken in conjunction with the three great encyclicals, *Mater et magistra, Pacem in terris,* and *Ecclesiam suam.* For an adequate idea of that ample teaching, it is necessary to go to the documents themselves. Here let us outline it rapidly, indicating only the broad headings.

The Church's doctrine starts with the affirmation of man's dual nature and his supernatural destiny. In all his activities, he must maintain the hierarchy of values which this destiny implies; in his entire earthly pilgrimage he must have his eyes fixed firmly on the "celestial city" which is his true home. To pursue the ends for which he has been created, he needs and claims liberty of conscience and liberty of person, and facilities for the pursuit of truth and the development of his complete personality—both his body and his mind. In this again the Church insists on the right order, the primacy of the spiritual and the intellectual over the material and the temporal. This implies, under modern conditions, freedom of information and facility for scientific research in every field. Next comes the teaching that concerns man as a social being. The family is the first and most natural social unit, and man has a right to everything that will ensure full and integral family life—the sacredness and stability of the marriage bond, the right to educate the children in the ideals in which he believes, the right to means of livelihood and to a family wage. This brings us to the immense field of Catholic teaching on socio-economic problems, the relations between capital and labour, the rights of the working classes, the right to private property both as the expression of justice and as the safeguard of liberty and as security for the family. But the evolution of modern industry and of economic theory has enabled the Church to define more clearly the limits and conditions of private ownership to the point of declaring the need, under certain conditions, to socialize property.

The last series of directives which I shall mention is also in some ways the latest to receive the attention of the magisterium of the Church—that which refers to the political and the international order. I have already said something about the nature and source of the power of the state, when speaking of democracy and the sovereignty of the people. The Church expresses no preference as to types of government. She insists that the function of the state is to ensure order and freedom in the temporal sphere and to promote the common good. The good of particular nations is not independent of the good of the world community, and so the Church approves and welcomes the growth of international organizations and the ensuring of peace by international agreements. She condemns racial discrimination and the colonial exploitation of subject nations; she affirms the moral obligation of the more prosperous nations to assist the underdeveloped countries. The preservation of peace in a world menaced by total destruction from nuclear war has become one of the greatest preoccupations of the Holy See, and there is no means of securing it without collective action.

From the "mustard seed" contained in the Gospel, the secular and social doctrine of the Church has developed into this mighty tree, its branches spreading over the entire human family in its present expansion and covering all the activities of its countless, complex, subsidiary societies and groups. There is in the evolution of this great body of teaching such continuity and logical sequence in all its diverse parts, such consistency and coherence in its relevance to the actual human condition, such compelling force, that only the presence of the Holy Spirit in the Church and his unfailing guidance can explain them.

There is a final point to be noted before we end this chapter. In speaking of the Church's present attitude to Protestantism and Protestant achievements, of liberty and tolerance, of the secular progress of modern man, it may seem (and in fact it has been said) that the Church was retracting her earlier condemnations and making radical changes in some of the doctrines she had formerly professed. This is a superficial judgement. There is a simple principle to help us to understand some of these apparent contradictions. When the rejected doctrines were first proposed, in the form in which they were proposed by the adversaries of the Church, their objective was to destroy the very notion, the prerogatives, and the system of government of the Church. That was the purpose of the Protestant appeal to the Bible, of the liberal insistence on liberty, and on separation of church and state. As we have seen, Protestantism and liberalism have evolved, and their activities have no longer the same old sectarian and anti-Catholic orientation. Their followers understand the Church much better. The Council, for its part, made an effort to clarify her own teaching, to expose and bring out all the doctrines and practical consequences flowing from the "mystery of the Church." So she can now modify her disapproval without compromising her integrity and doctrinal consistency. It is yet another example of how she takes up the best in human cultural development, divests it of its imperfections, stamps it with her own inner spirit, and makes it forever a part of her own ever-growing heritage.

CHAPTER IX

CATHOLIC RESTORATION:
THE NON-CHRISTIAN WORLD

We have already seen how the condemnation of the so-called Chinese and Malabar Rites caused a serious setback to the missions in China and India, and how the subsequent suppression of the Society of Jesus almost ruined a large number of prosperous mission stations. Many Catholic communities in all parts of the world where the Society had been doing mission work were left without pastors. The place of the Jesuits was taken by other religious orders and congregations, such as the Lazarists, Franciscans, and the Paris Society of Foreign Missions; but it was not possible for them to continue all the enterprises of the Jesuits. Some of the neglected communities reverted to their former religions. The growing unbelief in the Catholic countries which had sent out the largest number of missionaries, and the growth of the revolutionary spirit, diminished the number of missionary vocations.

In the meantime the great missionary effort characteristic of modern Protestantism was sending increasing numbers of devoted men and women to territories till then evangelized by Catholics exclusively, and they were making rapid progress. The Dutch Calvinists had, in an earlier period, started persecuting the Catholics in areas where they had acquired political power, as in Ceylon; or they had forbidden the entry of Catholic missionaries, as in Indonesia. Elsewhere, particularly in India, many neglected Catholics went over to Protestantism. Moreover, wars and political insecurity made mission work difficult in many areas. In a word, the Catholic missions at the time of the Revolution were in a pitiable condition.

The Catholic Restoration of the nineteenth century, however, brought with it a widely renewed missionary activity which has been growing and gathering strength ever since.[1] Many circumstances helped the renewal. There was first the restoration of many religious orders, notably of the Society of Jesus, which very quickly took up their work in many of their former missions in Asia, Africa, and America. There were also many new congregations—the Oblates of Mary Immaculate, the Salesians, the Society of the Divine Word, the Fathers of the Holy Ghost, the Pallottines, and others—who undertook widespread missionary works. What is even more important, congregations exclusively missionary, such as the White Fathers and the White Sisters, the Foreign Missionaries of Milan, and the African Missions of Lyons, began to be established in almost every country in Europe. Another circumstance which helped the new missionary activity was the dominion of European countries over the greater part of what are known as missionary territories; that is, territories where the large majority of people were non-Christians willing to receive missionaries and listen to the Gospel message. This was true of the Hindu, Buddhist, and Confucian people and generally for the populations of Asia and Africa but, except for Indonesia, less true of the Muslim countries where conversion on a big scale was practically impossible.

In general the colonial powers favoured the work of the missions, with a bias in favour of the missionaries of their own nationality and religion. The East India Company, anxious not to offend sensitive Hindu sentiment and determined to maintain religious neutrality, was at first opposed to missionary

[1] The reader will remember Macaulay's reference to Catholic missionaries in the passage quoted in Chapter VIII.

activity. But the English administrators realized before long that the missions rendered valuable service to the people, and so they not only permitted the apostolate but even indirectly encouraged it. The Dutch in Indonesia did not at first allow Catholic missionaries, and this gave a better start to the Protestants. The French and the Belgians, on the other hand, naturally favoured the Catholics.

Two special features of the modern missionary apostolate which have a bearing on our study must be noted here. First, the extraordinary development of educational works conducted by missionaries. They hoped by this means to spread the knowledge of the Gospel among the elite of the land and, through them, to convert the masses. Although they did not succeed in this objective and had to give up all attempts at direct proselytism in most of their schools, their educational work has had lasting consequences on the cultural evolution of the people of mission countries. In many of them—India, Indonesia, and African colonies of the European powers—such educational works were generally controlled and subsidized by the governments and were integrated with the official educational system of the country.

The other feature, also in keeping with the humanitarian and democratic spirit of the times, was the multiplication by missionary agencies of the works of social assistance: hospitals, orphanages, homes for the aged and the incurable, rescue homes, and leprosy sanitariums. The entire missionary work among primitive people in all the continents, and especially among the untouchables in India, had a social significance of the highest importance, as did the pioneer work of the missions for the education of women in many countries where the status of women was poor. In these two ways, the missionary apostolate of the nineteenth century acquired dimensions which went beyond the immediate objective of religious instruction and baptism. (This will receive greater attention later in this chapter when we speak of the "second phase" in the missionary revival.)

The exceptional advantages with which the modern missionary apostolate began—the indirect favour of the ruling colonial powers, the prestige of Western culture, the extensive educational and social works they undertook—gave hopes of vast movements of conversion among all classes in the mission countries. These hopes were fulfilled to some extent in Africa, but in the countries of ancient civilization—in China, Japan, Indonesia, India—the movement was slowed down, and among the educated elite almost stopped entirely, by the national and cultural revivals which began among these nations before the end of the nineteenth century. The very weapons which the missions had used to further the work of evangelization, as Western education and social assistance, were turned against them and made the objects of bitter attack as amounting to what was called "cultural aggression" and the securing of converts by the promise of material advantages. "Rice Christians" became the contemptuous description given by the adversaries of the missions to large sections of the Christian neophytes.

At the same time, under the inspiration of Western political ideals, movements of democracy and national independence started and developed rapidly in every subject country. The political resurgence was accompanied by revivals of national cultures and national religions. Often the leaders and heads of these religions, stung by the attacks of the missionaries, tried to introduce serious reforms and put their houses in order. They suppressed many of the social abuses which had been associated with their religion. Then they stirred up opposition against the missionaries by describing them as allies of the European powers in their colonial and imperial enterprises.[2]

---

[2] See *Asia and Western Dominance* by K. M. Panikkar, in which he makes a sustained attack on the Christian missions. The present

The national movements gathered momentum in the last years of the nineteenth century and the early years of the twentieth. World War I, "to make the world safe for democracy," gave them a mighty push. At the end of World War II it was clear that the former colonies and dominions of European powers could no longer be kept under subjection. It was feared that when independence came it would bring a general prohibition of missionary work or at least a severe control and limitation of it. Independence came in rapid succession to India, Burma, and Ceylon, to the Philippines and to Indonesia. China shook off all the vestiges of the humiliating concessions made to foreign powers in the great cities and commercial centres. Then followed the African colonies and, finally, what remained of colonial domination in Indo-China and Malaya. The Portuguese colonies, where Portugal still holds out, are distracted by clandestine liberation movements and local warfare.

The great and surprising turn in this attainment of independence by the former colonies is that, contrary to all fears, except in China, the missionary work has not been banned or seriously weakened. It is quite true that in many countries, in Asia particularly, there is opposition to foreign missionaries and severe control over their entry. This in its turn has intensified the effort to recruit a national clergy, with some disadvantages and many advantages to our missionary apostolate. In some places the status of the missions is better than it was when they worked under the foreign colonial administrators. Movements of conversions still go on and in certain places they attain the proportions of mass movements. As in Europe and America, the nineteenth-century Restoration of Christianity has its counterpart in the mission countries, and there, too, it reveals two

writer tried to answer Panikkar in a modest work, *Sardar Panikkar and Christian Missions* (1956).

phases. The second is still in process of evolution. It has not merely local importance but world-wide implications. We must now briefly indicate the reasons and the process of this remarkable transformation.

We must confess that the missionaries of the middle years of the nineteenth century, the Victorian period and the heyday of colonial rule, did tend to identify the Church and Western culture, or at least to present Western culture as being most favourable to her growth. It was a time when Europe had no suspicion of those weaknesses hidden in the heart of the Western socio-economic system which were laid bare later after the two world wars. In the earlier epoch there was a sense of exultation in the infinite capacity for progress which Europe seemed to possess, and the children of the ancient civilizations of Asia fell under the fascination of European culture and asked with avidity for Western education.[3] The rapid transformation of Japan under this impulse was an example to the rest of Asia. In these circumstances the older missionary traditions of studying the national cultures and adapting the Christian message to the psychological and cultural peculiarities of those people were partly neglected. Even the character of the people, their weakness and their strength, was judged by Western standards and conventions. As in the political sphere, so in the ecclesiastical, the higher posts were reserved for foreigners.

There was danger lest the Church be considered an alien institution, a religion good for the people of the West and not necessary for salvation to Asians. The Asian tendency to dogmatic indifferentism, and the theory that many religious could

[3] Let us recall the contemptuous terms in which Macaulay spoke of Indian beliefs and "scientific theories" in his famous *Minute on Education in India* by which the system of English education was introduced into India. Ram Mohun Roy, one of the makers of modern India, welcomed the decision with enthusiasm.

be "true" or at least equal in their aptitude to bring spiritual solace to their adepts, confirmed Asians—Indians in particular —in the belief that Christianity was a foreign religion. Thus, something of the conditions which had existed in Asia before the emergence of Ricci and De Nobili recurred in the mission field during this first phase. In the Catholic Church, however, there were many redeeming features: the presence of the descendants of the older converts in China and Japan, the existence of the Oriental Rites in some parts of Asia, notably in India, the continuation of some of the practices permitted by De Nobili in Madura. Leo XIII had re-established an Indian hierarchy among the Syro-Malabar Catholics of what is now known as Kerala. He had founded a great seminary for Indian priests in Kandy, Ceylon, and on that occasion had uttered the memorable words: "Thy own children, O India, will be ministers of salvation to thee."

After World War I, Benedict XV began an authoritative movement to "plant" the Church in the mission territories. The promotion of a national clergy and a national episcopate became a cardinal point in the missionary policy of Benedict XV and Pope Pius XI. The missionaries were urged to study the language, art, and culture of the peoples among whom they were working and of the country which, in a sense, they had made their own. They were warned not to publish in missionary journals descriptions and reflections on the miseries and deficiencies of the peoples of those countries which would be only partially true, and which in any case would wound their peoples' sensibilities. Encouragement was given to the architects, painters, artists, and musicians of the countries to adapt those arts to the expression of Christian doctrine and religious sentiment. The missionaries themselves felt reluctant to impose on the converts inferior imitations of European or Western art. Once again Catholic scholars were asked to study deeply and with sympathetic understanding the religious thought and literature of these countries as Ricci, De Nobili, and Beschi had done. And this not only with regard to the older civilizations of Asia, but also to the deep-rooted moral and religious sentiments hidden in the tribal cultures of Africa.[4]

All these directives are embodied in the great missionary documents of the last Popes, *Maximum illud* of Pope Benedict XV, *Rerum ecclesiae* of Pope Pius XI, *Evangelii precones* and *Fidei donum* of Pope Pius XII and *Princeps pastorum* of Pope John XXIII. They find their culmination in the Conciliar *Decree on the Missionary Activity of the Church,* in the *Declaration on Non-Christian Religions,* and in the establishment of a secretariate for non-Christian religions on the model of the secretariate for non-Catholic Christians. In these documents the theology of the missionary apostolate is authoritatively exposed and the practical policies to be followed in carrying out the mandate of the Church are also indicated in their broad outlines. In these policies, cultural adaptation and the need to avoid the identification of the Church with Western civilization has naturally an important place. Now let us see how the Church can take up the unfinished work of Ricci and De Nobili and resume their policy in the conditions of today.

The capital point to be retained here is that, while "adaptation" today cannot be simply an indiscriminate repetition of the experiments of the seventeenth-century pioneers, the guiding principle must remain the same. We have to present the Christian message in language and symbols which the non-Christians can understand and accept as being the realization of their own

[4] Cf. the well-known book of Father Placide Tempels, *Bantu Philosophy*. For the tribal culture of some of the Indian Adibasis (Aborigines), cf. Father Hoffman's monumental *Encyclopedia Mundarica*. For the Gonds, the chief authority is Dr. Verrier Elwin, an outstanding anthropologist. Dr. Elwin began his career as an Anglican missionary, but later developed a strong anti-missionary bias.

best aspirations, the fulfilment of their deepest needs. They should not be asked to enter into an alien world where psychologically and emotionally they cannot feel at home. Conversion must be a "coming home." And all this must be done without minimizing the essentially "revolutionary" nature of the Christian message. But it is a revolution to restore and fulfil, not to destroy and subvert.

Today, the changed cultural and religious conditions in the world and the evolution of Catholic theological thought have modified to a large extent the scope and spirit of that adaptation. Our attitude now to the non-Christian religions and the cultures which they have inspired, and in large measure created, should be determined in the light of three series of facts. We shall thus see that adaptation is not merely a question of missionary tactic, a concession to human weakness, but the fruit of a deeper understanding of the "mystery of Christ."

First, there is better knowledge and understanding of the great non-Christian religions. The scientific scholarship and critical sense of today have enabled the Christian world to see how beautiful, how lofty, some of the religious speculations and expressions of religious devotion are in those religions. We see that there have been men of the highest probity and devotion among their followers. Even while admitting the vast difference between them and the authentic Christian saints with their heroic virtue, we are no longer shocked in seeing some of them—Muslims, Hindus, Buddhists—called "saints" and holy men. We realize that the grace of God has been working in them in some mysterious way. We know that in the actual economy of salvation there is no grace given to man which is not the grace of Christ. Christ died for all men and his will is that all men should be saved. Hence, the Church asserts, and now repeats in the clearest terms in the conciliar documents, that those who aspire after truth and goodness and live according to the dictates of their conscience, but ignore the message of the Gospel through no culpable fault of their own, will be saved by the grace of Christ.

As we have already seen, however, according to another accepted doctrine, "outside the Church there is no salvation." Hence these men are said to belong to the soul of the Church, not to its visible body. Karl Rahner calls them "anonymous Christians." Teilhard de Chardin speaks (in *The Divine Milieu*) of the "Diaphany" of Christ, the hidden presence in the universe of him in whom all things were created and all things restored. If the Epiphany is the public manifestation of Our Lord, and if our open adhesion to his person by membership of the visible Church is a participation in the mystery of the Epiphany, then the hidden adhesion of those who belong to the soul of the Church should be a participation in his Diaphany. It is certainly an arresting concept.

It is not difficult to give examples in non-Christian religions of this aspiration towards Christ, and the reaching out by the instincts of human nature itself to some of the external forms and ceremonies by which Our Lord communicates grace to souls in the Sacraments. Thus the use of ablutions as symbols of spiritual purification, of sacramental meals as symbols of intimate union with the divinity, are found in many religions both primitive and advanced. The Hindus have had from very early times the concept of some kind of Incarnation or *Avatar* of God. In the *Bhagavad Gita*, in which non-Christian religion seems to attain one of its noblest expressions, there is the moving evocation of a god of love and grace who grants salvation to his devotees in response to the simplest expression of their love—even the offering of a leaf or a flower. This is very different from the exacting of strict retribution of their misdeeds according to the accepted Hindu doctrine of Karma. This god of love and grace is said to take human form to teach and guide mankind whenever some great need or crisis arises.

In Mahayana Buddhism there is the example of the Bodhi-sattvas—reincarnations of the Buddha—who, by the purity and perfection of their lives, secure the right to be freed from the cycle of rebirths and attain eternal nirvana; but they deliberately choose to be reborn on earth out of love for man and the desire to help them in their sufferings. Professor R. C. Zaehner[5] describes this "tremendous vow of the Bodhisattva not to enjoy the eternal bliss that is within his grasp but to accept a bitter crucifixion on the cross of the world until all souls enter before him into the peace of nirvana" as perhaps "the most grandiose ideal that the Indian mind has ever conceived." Because of this, as well as of those features of the *Bhagavad Gita* which I have indicated, he considers the men who proclaimed those teachings as being the "prophets outside Israel" whom St. Paul may have had in mind when he said that God had spoken "at sundry times and in many ways to mankind before speaking in these latest times through his Son" (Hebrews 1:1).

Perhaps I should mention here the remarkable case of conversion to the Catholic faith of an evangelical Protestant missionary, William Wallace, whose experience of Hindu religious practices, the place that concepts and practices similar to those of Catholicism had in their lives—such as ceremonial worship, sacramentalism, pilgrimages, asceticism, and the monastic ideal, etc.—led him to reject the Reformation and enter the Catholic Church.[6]

So much for the first series of facts. A second consideration is the certainty that, before the modern missionary penetra-

[5] *At Sundry Times* by R. C. Zaehner. Zaehner is Spalding Professor of Eastern Religions at the University of Oxford and is a convert to Catholicism.
[6] Father Wallace became a Jesuit and died as a missionary in India. The story of his conversion is narrated in his fascinating *From Evangelical to Catholic by Way of the East.*

tion, there were Christian religious contacts with the non-Christian world and Christian influence on the religious ideas and practices of those people. Thus, in Islam there is not only an indebtedness to the Old Testament and the Hebraic revelation since the Muslims accept the historicity of the books of the Old Testament and the promise of a Messiah, but there is also the direct indebtedness to Christianity insofar as Our Lord is accepted as the greatest prophet before Mohammed and the Blessed Virgin is given such exceptional honour that often the words of the Koran have been interpreted as insinuating the doctrine of the Immaculate Conception. Then there is the fair probability of the influence of Nestorian Christianity on the Lammaist sects of Mahayana Buddhism. Their ceremonies, specially in the Lammaist monasteries of Tibet, are so similar to Christian liturgical ceremonies, and the fact of the penetration of Nestorian missionaries in these regions is now so well established, that many scholars are convinced of considerable borrowing from the latter.

But the most impressive testimony regarding such early Christian influence on non-Christian religions is the development of the Bhakti cult in India. We saw that the *Bhagavad Gita*, which admittedly is a product of the pre-Christian era—at least two hundred years before Our Lord—contains the first announcement of the cult of a God of grace and love. But this seed initially remained almost sterile, to burst forth into vigorous life centuries later through the *Vaishnava* movement initiated by Ramanuja and Madhava in South India. Chaitanya and Ramananda introduced it in Bengal, Namdev and Tukaram in Maharashtra. Between the eleventh and sixteenth centuries it inspired a rich devotional literature in the different regional languages wherein the worship of an incarnate god, Krishna or Rama, is preached in language and contains incidents so manifestly Christian that it is difficult to believe that they are mere coincidences. Rama, for instance, is said to retain his human personality after his ascent into heaven—a feature quite opposed to Hindu concepts. Krishna is described as washing the feet of his disciples. There are legends of Madhava and other Bhaktas walking over the sea, of the cutting off of arms and plucking out of eyes that have offended, of turning the other cheek when smitten on one. The probability of the Christian source of these resemblances becomes a certainty when we recall that the initiators of the Bhakti movement, Ramanuja and Madhava, were born and brought up in places where there were communities of Christians—Mylapore near Madras, and Kalyan on the west coast of India. Sir George Grierson, unequalled in his knowledge of the languages and religious history of India, passed this unequivocal judgement on the Christian influence on the Bhakti movement:

> Although the conceptions of the Fatherhood of God and Bhakti were indigenous to India, they received an immense impetus owing to the beliefs of Christian communities reacting upon the medieval Bhagawata reformers of the South. With this leaven their teaching swept over Hindustan bringing balm and healing to a nation gasping in its death throes amid the horrors of alien invasion.[7] It is not overstating the case to say that in this reformation India rediscovered faith and love, and the fact of this discovery accounts for the passionate enthusiasm of the contemporary religious writings. In them we behold the profoundest depths of the human heart laid bare with a simplicity and freedom from self-consciousness unsurpassed in any literature with which the writer is acquainted.[8]

[7] Allusion to the Muslim invasions and conquest of northern India. Mahummud of Ghazni began the first of his seventeen invasions in 1001. The country knew no peace till Akbar ascended the throne in 1556.

[8] *Encyclopedia of Religion,* article "Bhakti," II, 550.

Passing now to the modern period, we come to the third consideration, namely the effect of the missionary apostolate on the non-Christian religions and the penetration of Christian ideas among them even when they did not accept Christianity in its totality. This effect has been so manifold in its expressions, so varied in the different religious, social, and political conditions where it was felt, that it is impossible to summarize it adequately. Let us first note the impact of Christian preaching on primitive religions in Africa and in some parts of Asia, and even in America.

The knowledge of the social and political ideals of the West, which Western education and the contact with the Western world had given to people under European domination, led, as we noted, to national movements for democracy and independence. When the missionaries preached the Gospel to these subject peoples, the latter were at the same time undergoing a political awakening. So in many places those who heard the missionaries or became even nominally Christian took up some of the elements of Christian teaching, combined them with their older beliefs, and created syncretist movements in which the notion of a leader or messiah who was to deliver his people from subjection assumed a very important place. These examples of religio-political prophetism have been an important feature of the first stages of their struggle for political emancipation. We see this in the Boxer movement in China, in Indo-China, in Indonesia, even in India among many primitive or Adibasi tribes, among the Negroes and Indians of America, and to a notable extent in Africa.

Among the Muslims the influence in the line of prophetism was less pronounced. The chief example of it seems to have been Mirza Ghulam Ahmed, the founder of the Quadianite sect, who claimed that since he came "in the spirit and power of Jesus" the prophecy of the second coming was fulfilled in him. The principal effect of the missionary challenge on Islam was the movement of social reform—the emancipation of women, the abolition of slavery. The cult of the Prophet Mohammed, a type of personal cult alien to primitive Islam, owes a good deal to the place given to Our Lord in the Christian economy.

In primitive Buddhism (*Hinayana* or *Theravada*) there is no room for a personal god or a saviour. But we have already seen how in popular, or Mahayana, Buddhism the doctrine of the *Bodhisattva* brings in an element which has many analogies with Christian teaching. In the present-day revivalism of Buddhism, especially as it is presented to the West, the absence of a personal god and the rejection of the idea of creation is particularly emphasized. In this way its leaders wish to prove that there is no opposition between Buddhism and modern science. They make no secret of their hopes of making Buddhism the religion of the intellectual classes of the future. Even modern "aggressive" Buddhism, however, has not hesitated to assimilate the social ideals of Christianity and to imitate Christian organizations in their missionary methods.

Nevertheless, in Japan, the new cults, variations of Buddhism or of Shinto, which have pullulated after Japan's defeat in World War II, the syncretism, which we noted in primitive religions, is much in evidence and many points of Christian doctrine and practice are seen in them. Even Zen Buddhism, which attaches itself to the *Hinayana*, is adopting more and more the idea of a mediator-helper for attaining salvation. Arnold Toynbee, after a recent visit to Japan, says this of the religious situation there:

What about the prospects of Christianity in the new Japan which is now painfully struggling to be born? Japanese Christians occupy eminent posts today, but they are, of course, no more than a tiny minority, and it seems improbable that there will be further conversions on any large scale. At the same time it looks as if the spirit of Christianity were permeating Japanese life and were beginning gradually to replace or transform the traditional influence of Buddhism. On the conscious surface of the mind the present painful groping may long continue. But deeper down, at the subconscious level, the Japanese people may already be finding the bread of life.[9]

It is in India and in Hinduism that we see the widest evidence of the influence of missionary preaching in modern times. After the first great wave of conversions among all classes, Hinduism stiffened itself to resist the attack and to put its own house in order. Important movements of social and religious reform were initiated, all more or less revealing the influence of Christianity.[10] The most notable among them was the *Brahmo Samaj*, a form of reformed Hinduism which did away with caste and rebirth and taught a strict monotheism. The greatest of the *Brahmo Samaj* leaders, Keshab Chandra Sen, was an ardent admirer and lover of Jesus. Another leader, Maharishi Debendranath Tagore, the father of Rabindranath, was less influenced by Christianity, though in his autobiography it is said that his favourite prayer to God was a Bengali translation of a prayer composed by Fénelon. The other Hindu reformed groups, such as the *Arya Samaj*, the Theosophical Society, the Ramakrishna Mission, though unfriendly and sometimes aggressive in their attitude to Christianity, accepted a large measure of social reform based on Christian ideas—partly as a reaction to the missionary attacks on Hinduism. J. N. Farquhar quotes Sir Narayan Chandavarkar, a distinguished jurist, as summing up this aspect of modern Hinduism: "The ideas that lie at the heart of the Gospel of

[9] *East to West—A Journey Around the World* (O.U.P., 1958).
[10] They are described in J. N. Farquhar's fascinating *Modern Religious Movements in India.*

Christ are slowly but surely permeating every part of Hindu society and modifying every phase of Hindu thought."[11]

In the same line, there is another development very characteristic of India and her syncretist spirit: not merely the acceptance of the social and ethical ideas of Christianity, but the cult of Jesus himself and his Blessed Mother, the readiness to accept him as an incarnate divinity, though not the unique one. Knowledge of the New Testament is common among all educated Hindus, and they quote the Gospel frequently, freely, reverently. The highest praise they could give to Mahatma Gandhi was to say that he was "Christ-like."[12] In one of the most famous temples of south India I have seen Hindu vendors selling medals of the sacred heart manufactured by Hindu craftsmen. When I asked them what they represented, one of them replied with a smile: "That is the Lord of the Divine Heart" (*Thivvya Irudayanather*). In India there are many shrines of Our Lady. The most famous of them are at Bandra in Bombay and at Vellangany on the east coast not far from Negapatam. Of the thousands of visitors and pilgrims who frequent these shrines the majority are Hindus, Parsees, and Muslims. That is an indication of the degree in which Christian beliefs have entered into the religious consciousness of the people of India.

Lastly, let us remember that this slow penetration of Christian ideas and practices is taking place in the wider setting of the diffusion of Western civilization as a whole all over the world—its social and political ideals, its scientific spirit, its educational organization, its technical inventions, its sports and recreations. They come to a large extent in a secular guise, and

[11] *Op. cit.*

[12] Mahatma Gandhi was assassinated on a Friday. For many Hindus this was one more proof of his resemblance to Jesus. Others thought that he might be a "reincarnation" of Christ.

bring with them much evil along with the good. But let us remember that the best elements in them, the nucleus of ideas and attitudes that have gone to the creation of Western civilization, had Christian origins and have a Christian resonance. This part of the modern world-wide civilization joins hands with Christianity, and to that extent it is an ally of the preachers of Christianity. This is no longer the imposition of Western dominance by foreigners, but the willing acceptance by the people of the permanent values of Western civilization.

Because of this direct and indirect penetration of Christianity into non-Christian societies, it would be right to say that the world is being slowly "Christianized" in a broad sense. This is a fact of capital importance. Those who must adapt the Christian message to the culture and temperaments of the non-Christian peoples must take full cognizance of it. It makes their task somewhat different from that of Ricci and De Nobili; it makes it easier in some ways, but in others more difficult, and calls for greater subtlety of understanding and greater flexibility in practice.[13]

---

[13] It was obviously not the scope of this chapter to give a detailed account of the missionary work and of the condition of the missions today. I have chosen only those details that have a bearing on the question of cultural adaptation.

CHAPTER X

DUC IN ALTUM

"When he had finished speaking he said to Simon, stand out in the deep water and let down your nets for a catch. Simon answered him, Master, we have toiled all the night, and caught nothing, but at thy word I will let down the net. And when they had done this, they took a great quantity of fish so that the net was near breaking." (Luke, Ch. 5, 4-7)

It is the mission of Paul VI in the post-Conciliar Church to incarnate in himself the spirit of the Council, and by his authority and action to complete the Council's task. He is called upon to end the isolation of the Church in the modern world, and take the bark of Peter out onto the open sea. At this crucial period of history, the task of promoting the universal mission of the Church has been committed to him by Catholic Christendom which desired and awaited his election as pope. He comes to it with singular aptitude because of his background and because of the training he has received. His family has taken an important part in the public life of the Italian nation, and in the efforts of the Catholics of the country to mould that life in accordance with the social and moral teaching of the Church. He has been intimately associated with the work of Pius XI and Pius XII, and hence was in touch with the new spirit in the government of the Church, with her determination to secure a hearing in the great world, and had a part in the shaping of events that affect all humanity. We have seen that the *aggiornamento,* which Pope John XXIII made the watchword of his own policy and the motto of the Council, had begun after World War I under Benedict XV, but more particularly under his two successors. Monsignor Montini was the collaborator of both of them and, more intimately, the helper and virtual Secretary of State of Pius XII.

This close association with Pius XI and Pius XII has not prevented him from entering with sympathetic understanding into the spirit of Pope John, who esteemed him, trusted him, and, foreseeing perhaps with something more than human foresight the future role he was to play, prepared him for what was to come. A scholar by instinct and preference, master of many languages, a passionately interested reader of books on the thought and spirit of contemporary man, it was actually feared that his intellectual cast of mind might not fit him for the incessant action which the situation of the post-Conciliar Church called for. Not a few papers, indulging in a facile cliché, called him a "Hamlet" in the first months of his pontificate. But we do not hear this any more. The uninterrupted activity of this frail man during these two years—the number, the promptness, and the force of his comments on public events, the courage of his many initiatives—have astonished the world. His helpers and ministers can scarcely keep pace with him. In truth, he seems to be carried forward irresistibly by the force of the spirit. I have seen him in India among those immense surging crowds, at certain moments almost disarmed and helpless because of his utter goodness and readiness to "spend himself." In a deeper sense, in his entire career as pope of the post-Conciliar Church, he seems "disarmed" and hurried along by the mighty wind of this new Pentecost.

Let us cast a quick glance at what Pope Paul has done during the two years of his pontificate to open the windows and send out the message of the Church and the Council to the principal categories of men who stand around the Church. They are ranged in widening circles farther and farther away from the centre, as he himself has described. First, his ecumenical action. Foremost in this line comes the meeting with Patriarch Athenagoras in Jerusalem, their kiss of peace, followed by many gestures of mutual friendliness and ending in the historical decision of the two churches to withdraw the mutual excommunications which had kept the Roman and the Orthodox Church in a state of permanent disaccord. All the time, thanks to the work of his admirable Secretariate for Non-Catholic Christians and its unwearying President, Cardinal Bea, the relations with the Holy Synod, with the Patriarchate of Russia, and with the Protestant World Council of Churches, have become more intimate. Ways of mutual consultation and cooperation in social and charitable undertakings with some of them have been established. To give one example, a recent conference on the lay apostolate, held in Rome to prepare for the World Congress in 1967, was attended by observers from the World Council of Churches, from the YMCA, and from the YWCA. They took as much part in the discussions as the Catholic delegates and made some very interesting and useful contributions.

The latest example of inter-church relations was the visit to Rome of Dr. Ramsey, the Archbishop of Canterbury. Lord Fisher, Dr. Ramsey's predecessor at Canterbury, has recalled in a letter to the press how his own earlier visit was given as little publicity and solemnity as possible. This visit of Dr. Ramsey was made in an altogether different atmosphere and in a different manner. The head of the Anglican Church and his entourage were received with the solemnity accorded to heads of state. His meetings with the pope ended with a common service of prayer and intercession in St. Paul's Outside the Walls in which the pope took part. Paul's last gesture was dramatic and utterly unexpected: he took off his own episcopal ring and put it on the archbishop's finger. It was the symbol of a historic reconciliation.

I referred to the pope's meeting with Patriarch Athenagoras in Jerusalem. The main purpose of that pilgrimage was to follow the steps of Our Lord, to enter more fully into his mind and the dispositions of his heart by communing with him in prayer in the setting of the land where he had once walked. It was natural that one who was trying with all the resources of his spirit to penetrate more deeply into the mystery of the Church should want to come into closer contact in this way also with the historical Jesus. In the spots hallowed by his life and Passion, by the Risen Life, by his supreme command to go and preach to all nations, and by the coming of the Holy Spirit, Paul could contemplate the source and the beginnings of the Church. That was the primary impulse behind the dramatic decision to go to the Holy Land. But there were other contacts of profound significance to be made there.

On this sacred soil he was going to meet the authoritative representatives of three great categories of men with whom the Church was seeking to achieve reconciliation and friendship: the Jews, whose alienation from the Christian peoples had its roots in the divine tragedy which had taken place here; the Muslims, whose age-old rivalry and enmity with the Christian nations had been sharpened by the Crusaders' attempts to conquer this land; the Orthodox Greeks, whose separation from the Church became wider and deeper because of the bitter events connected with those Crusades, above all by the capture and the sack of Constantinople in 1257. Surely these historical memories must have crowded on the scholarly mind of Paul VI, and his pastor's heart must have felt deeply the providential encounter with the representatives of these three forces, once adverse to the Church, and now brought near by the power of the Spirit and the light of a new vision. It was fitting that Jerusalem should be the ground on which these reconciliations, inspired by the spirit of Christ, should be initiated and started on the way, to become stronger and firmer in the future years.

Next came the momentous visit to India. It represented his contact not only with the people of India but, as he said, with the ancient peoples of the whole of Asia on the threshold of which he was standing, peoples of whose diversity he was getting a first experience in India. He had gone there with misgivings because of reports in the press which, in the last days before the journey, had spoken much of the opposition of the Hindu revivalists to the pope's journey. These revivalists are people who resent the missionary apostolate of the Church. Unlike the wiser political leaders of the country, they had not realized that the missionaries were precious auxiliaries of the nation even from the temporal point of view, educating the tradition-bound masses of the country in the techniques and spirit of the modern age. But all these misgivings were swept away by the unbelievable warmth of the welcome the holy father received. By hundreds of thousands the people turned out to greet him. The crowds that lined the streets from Santa Cruz airport to the Eucharistic Congress grounds in the heart of Bombay have been estimated at two million. They came to see not a foreign dignitary but a man of God, the "Holy Man of the West," whose *darshan*, or vision, they sought with religious fervour. Paul VI sensed this as he looked at their glowing eyes and outstretched hands.

The theologians of the Church in their pondering over the mystery of Jesus and of the Church had, as we saw, perceived the action of the grace of Jesus in souls outside the visible body of the Church. Possibly this visit to India and the contact with the Hindu people enabled the pope to touch, as it were with his finger, this aspect of the mystery of the Church. After his return to Rome, in his Christmas message to the world, he said this:

We went as a stranger and a pilgrim to a distant and unknown land; we might have remained there a stranger, isolated, surrounded only by our brothers in the Faith. But instead we came into contact with a people—innumerable, festive, overflowing. . . . There was a moment of understanding, of mingling of spirits. We saw in them a people ancient and young at the same time; today alert, and with looks turned towards something which even the tremendous modern progress cannot give, nay, might even obstruct.

The Eucharistic Congress itself was an achievement of superb organization. The Church of India seemed anxious to demonstrate to the Catholic world her ability to carry out such a grandiose manifestation as well as the Western nations could; and it succeeded. What did not sufficiently appear was the "Indian-ness" that was expected—the art and the spirit of India, her burning problems and the relevance of the faith and of the Eucharist in the solution of those problems "here and now." But that deficiency, if it existed, was made up for by the attitude and the words of the holy father. He pursued his "ecumenical mission" with single-minded devotion; he met the representatives of the non-Catholic Churches, including the ancient Jacobite Syrian Church; and those of the non-Christian religions—Hindus, Muslims, Parsees. In solemn public discourses he spoke of the age-old religious quest of India and illustrated his thought by striking quotations from the *Upanishads*. In one speech, he cited the words of the *Mundaka Upanishad*, "The truth shall always prevail"; and then, bridging the interval of twenty-five centuries, he quoted the beautiful hymn of Rabindranath Tagore, "Day after day, O Lord of my life, shall I behold Thee face to face," showing how apt it was before the ever-abiding presence of Jesus in the Eucharist. A few gestures, a few words. But they helped to put out the fires of many ancient controversies, and to dispel the doubts in many minds.

As an example of this I should like to cite a few words from a remarkable broadcast (on All-India Radio) made by one of the leading Hindu leaders of India, a close disciple and intimate friend of Mahatma Gandhi, Acharya Kalelkar:

> As a believing Hindu I was very happy that Pope Paul came to India. My happiness was justified by the pope's noble utterances in which he included a reference to Upanishadic prayers, and by his love for our people irrespective of their religion.

Then explaining that many Buddhists, Hindus, Muslims have their own fears that the ecumenical movement might be a veiled attempt to unite all Christians in order to dominate the non-Christian world, the Acharya continued:

> It has been my endeavour to persuade these alarmist elements to drop their fears. . . . With this attitude of mine I am greatly encouraged when my Christian friends assure me . . . that the Lord Christ came not to destroy but to fulfil; not to be served but to serve; that genuine Christianity is no warring conquest and subjugation but a charity-born brotherly effort to offer to all peoples a share in the spirit of Christ, as exhibited in the Sermon on the Mount and—barring possible abuses by mischievous elements which true Christianity sincerely regrets and repudiates—this has no implication whatever of political domineering. I wholeheartedly accept this assurance, and as a token of good will on our side, we sincerely acknowledge our deep debt of gratitude to the many missionaries—men and women—whose religiously inspired and dedicated lives have been spent in the service of our people.

The next dramatic journey of the pope was to New York to address the General Assembly of the United Nations, to establish a direct contact with the representatives of over 150 nations and to speak to them of peace—of the utter need for it, and of the desire of the Church to cooperate with every effort of the nations to promote it. It was also further and conclusive evidence of the Holy See's appreciation of the United Nations which, in spite of its imperfections, the Church regards as a necessary instrument for peace and cooperation among the nations. The UN was passing through a crisis, and the visit might have been intended, and in reality did much, to raise that organization's prestige. This was in keeping with the social teaching of the Church and in accord with the wishes of the Vatican Council. Hence Pope Paul, returning from New York, went straight to St. Peter's to speak to the assembled fathers of the memorable visit. And he directed that his speech to the UN should be included among the proceedings of the Council.

There is yet another development in this area of establishing contacts with the world which we owe to the energy and to the great personal humility of Pope Paul VI. He has not only maintained the custom begun by John XXIII of visiting the churches of Rome on the Sundays of Lent, speaking and moving among the people in a simple and unconstrained way; he has also begun visits on weekdays to particular groups of workers. One day he met the *netturbini,* the Roman street sweepers, a humble and hard-working group whose task is very difficult and unattractive; another time, a group of masons and workers engaged in construction; a third time, the employees of a great pharmaceutical manufacturer. To every group he addressed words inspired by understanding and appreciation of the work they were doing and affection for their persons and families. He said once with engaging frankness: "I am told that many of you do not go to church. So, since I cannot meet you there, I have come to see you." These visits are made in his capacity as Bishop of Rome. But at the same time he is engaged in "dialogue" with those who have broken away from the Church and have perhaps lost their faith. He knew that among the thousands who heard and cheered him there were many who were card-holding members of the Communist Party of Italy, the largest Communist party in the West.

In another important sphere of modern activity, the world of scientific research, Paul VI has further developed the contacts established by Pius XI (who founded the Pontifical Academy of Sciences) and continued by Pius XII. Its members now include scientists from all continents and from all religions, including Islam, Hinduism, and Buddhism. As we have seen, the Vatican Council has spoken of science and technology with understanding and admiration. Among the messages sent out by the holy father in the closing ceremony of the Council, there was one addressed to the intellectuals of the world. It was therefore in keeping with this spirit that in April, 1966, the Nuncio in Paris and the Papal Observer to UNESCO organized a conference of scientists and intellectuals—specialists in a great variety of subjects—to discuss the cultural implications of the decrees of the Council. The meeting was presided over by Dr. René Mahieu, director general of UNESCO. Protestant, Jewish, and Muslim participants brought out the contribution made by the Council to promote genuine humanism. Dr. Mahieu concluded by saying that this most successful conference had shown the harmony between the ideals of UNESCO and some of the pronouncements of the Council.

A few days after this, the Papal Academy of Sciences held in Rome its annual study week, this year consecrated to "Molecular Forces." At the end of the week, the holy father received them in audience and told them of his deep interest in the work of the academy. He then dwelt on the relations between science and religion, referring to the importance of the *Constitution on the Church in the Modern World.* He praised the spirit and objectives of scientific research, the high intelligence and strong moral qualities required to attain success in it. But he indicated the dangers to a universal outlook from overspecialization in limited fields. He reminded them that even the highest physical sciences left unanswered ultimate questions: the design of God, the demands of the moral law, the why and the wherefore of creation. The entire speech is a complement to the conciliar constitution.

This incessant activity of Paul VI and his predecessors, their desire to enter sympathetically into the restless and ever-changing aspects of contemporary civilization, should not, however, lead us to believe that the outlook of Catholicism is changed in essential points, and that, in particular, the Catholic insistence on piety, on prayer and interior life, on the role of what have been called the "passive virtues" in the ideal of Christian perfection has been modified in favour of some type of "activism." The very basis of any genuine Catholic apostolate is faith in supernatural means and union with God. The active and dynamic Pius XI surprised the non-Catholic world by declaring Patroness of the Missions a contemplative nun who died young and unknown in an obscure convent of France—St. Thérèse of the Child Jesus. The first act of Pope John after convoking the Council was to introduce the name of St. Joseph in the canon of the Mass, thus marking one more stage in the long process by which "the saint of the hidden life" has entered into the life and consciousness of Catholic Christendom.

Similarly, at every stage of the Church's expansion, devotion to Our Lady has received some new expression or special manifestation. Pius XII defined the dogma of the Assumption. Paul VI, to the surprise of many, and even the distress of some who feared that the step might wound Protestant susceptibilities in this era of ecumenism, declared Our Lady "Mother of the Church." But it was a logical and inevitable step. The

Council, reflecting on the nature and prerogatives of the Church, had affirmed with new force and clarity its primary note of being the mystical body of Christ, perpetuating the presence and ministry of Jesus on earth. It follows, therefore, that the mother of Jesus is the mother of the Church. Every step in the understanding of the mystery of Jesus has brought a better understanding of the place of Our Lady in the economy of salvation.

So we find Paul VI unflagging in his exhortations to piety and prayer. He prepared every one of the sessions of the Council with a veritable crusade of prayer and penance, the last session with a solemn penitential procession to the Church of the Holy Cross. Every Sunday he addresses the crowds in St. Peter's Square before the Angelus, bringing to their attention some emergent need or special intention of the Church and asking them to join him in praying to the mother of God and mother of men to obtain that grace.

We may confidently expect Pope Paul to carry out the decisions of the Council and remain scrupulously faithful to its spirit. But he will do this in a balanced and harmonious way, putting first things first and not pushing one side forward without heed to the rest. The people of "one idea" who are ready to pronounce the Council a failure and the pope indifferent to his responsibilities if *their* idea is not implemented at once will get no comfort or encouragement from Paul VI. Nor will those who are in a hurry be satisfied on all counts, in spite of the manifest sense of urgency under which the pope is spending himself without thought of rest. When he postponed the voting on the *Declaration on Religious Freedom,* these people pronounced the action a device to shelve the whole question. Otherwise, what leader with such a crushing majority at his disposal would have hesitated to ask for a vote? They forget that the pope is not the leader of a victorious majority party in a parliament but the father of Christendom whose care should be not to "scandalize" the least of his children.[1] So, as long as there is a chance of gaining over some of those who are opposed to a measure, either doctrinally or practically, the pope will bide his time, negotiate with infinite patience, and try to carry every one with him even at the price of minor concessions. He will and must try to do this. Neither he nor the Church as a whole can forget that after Vatican I a part of the minority that did not want papal infallibility did not accept the decision, and that the Church still suffers from the wound inflicted on her by the defection of Döllinger. Pope Paul, in his own way, succeeded in getting the document on religious freedom voted on with greater unanimity and less opposition from those still unconvinced.

It was said that when the Council and its commissions were at work with their hundreds of experts and were grappling with great problems of philosophy and theology, Rome had become the intellectual capital of the world. The post-conciliar commissions continue something of the same activity. It is fitting that they should do so under the guidance of a man with Paul VI's wide scholarship and quite exceptional intellectual energy. It is this strongly intellectual cast of mind which makes it impossible for him to come to decisions which have not been studied and reflected on in the most thoroughgoing fashion. They are "thought out" in the fullest sense of the term. The world of modern journalism, on the other hand, lives on the drama of swiftly moving daily events and is accustomed to their rapidity and variety. It does not, therefore, always understand what it calls the "delays and hesitations" of papal policy.

[1] Even in secular parliaments, let us remember, the majority party after the first voting on a proposed law submits it to a "select committee" which includes members of the opposition. The law may be passed by a majority, but it has to be obeyed by the whole country, including the opposition. Hence the need to obtain some kind of consensus.

In reality, the pope, too, has a sense of the dramatic. As we have seen, he can act swiftly and decisively. He has the widest interests and broadest sympathies; he can enter into the point of view of those who do not agree with him. That is one more reason why he should measure his words and leave many things unsaid. Such men are liable to be misunderstood and destined to suffer in silence. Therefore the mark of the Cross is on Paul, this "servant of Christ." It may well be that by that sign he will bring an unbelieving world closer to the "mystery of the Cross."

EPILOGUE

"ON WHITHER AND HOW"

In one of the last poems he wrote, "At the Hensbridge Cross at the Year's End," Thomas Hardy asked:

> Why go any road now?
> White stands the handpost for brisk onbearers,
> "Halt!" is the word for wancheeked farers,
> Musing on Whither and How.

Those lines express the profound pessimism which is modern unbelief's saddest legacy to its votaries.[1] Against that despairing creed, Charles Péguy has evoked the vision of Christian hope in one of the most characteristic productions of the Catholic Restoration, *Le Porche du Mystère de la deuxième Vertu*. The believer knows that history has a sense; that the designs of God are being worked out in the human story perfectly, though not always in a manner clear to us. It is in that spirit of faith and hope that I take up the words of Hardy to ask humbly and reverently whither the Church of God is moving today in the pursuit of her God-given mission.

Our inquiry has brought us to the present day. We have traced the action of the Church, her efforts to understand and enter into the secular cultural activity of her sons and to in-

---

[1] Hardy, however, was not without his own nostalgia for the beliefs which he no longer held. In the "Impercipient" he laments that he should be a stranger "to the bright believing band."

form it with her own spirit down the centuries. We have seen
it as a dynamic process marked by successive stages of development, each stage showing an enlarging and widening of the
scope of her action. It is therefore natural for us to look at the
future and try to see how this action will develop in some of
the major areas where she finds herself especially involved
at the present day.

Let us take the ecumenical movement first. The growth of
ecumenism, its recent swift and dramatic developments, are
—for those who see these things with the eye of faith—a manifest sign of the action, the well-nigh miraculous action, of the
Holy Spirit. Therefore it is hardly possible for a Catholic to
think that the movement will not at some time reach its term
and attain its objectives. The obstacles are still formidable, but
if we think of those which have been overcome in the recent
past, if we note that we are today doing things—e.g., common
religious services in which popes and archbishops and patriarchs of the separated churches participate—which even five
years ago seemed unthinkable, it is not too much to hope that
the remaining obstacles will likewise be overcome. Reunion,
with the Orthodox and the Episcopal churches at least, seems
no longer merely a dream.

If that happens, the cultural traditions that have grown and
ramified in these churches will be brought within the Catholic
sphere. The concept of what constitutes an authentic Christian
culture will again be enlarged and diversified. Such a diversi-
fication is indispensable for the universal message of the
Church as she goes on widening her boundaries.

Obviously this will be even truer in the measure that the
Church comes into contact with the world of Islam, Hinduism,
and Buddhism. We have seen what an enriching of the cultural heritage of the Church "adaptation" has already brought
to her in Asia and now in Africa. The further growth of the
Church among the followers of these great religions will bring

with it an even greater and more significant enrichment, and that in a twofold manner.

First, the liturgical changes will bring directly within the worship of the Church many new artistic patterns and devotional forms. While it is true that the dominance of the Latin language in the studies and worship of the Latin Church—the one chiefly involved in missionary work among non-Christian peoples—did not signify the identification of the Church with Western culture; nevertheless, that predominance created a very powerful link with the spirit and modes of Western culture. The liturgical changes weaken that link. They are a recognition of national cultures even in the Western world whose roots are Greco-Latin. They are more urgently needed and have been more heartily welcomed in the churches of Asia and Africa. In some of these regions it is not fanciful to foresee the emergence of fully constituted new rites in languages hitherto not used for the essential parts of liturgical worship.[2]

There is, however, another direction in which the encounter with the non-Christian religions and the inevitable give-and-take of "adaptation" might affect the thinking of Catholics in a way salutary for Western Christians. Those religions, remaining as they have done in a less "advanced" environment, have preserved values and attractions which the secular tendencies of Western civilization have jeopardized even among Catholics. Thus, the Muslims give a magnificent example of brotherliness among all the followers of the Prophet, a challenge to Christians to revive the charity of primitive times. Better still, they have a consistency and a sincerity in bringing their religious principles into secular life which is very different from the

[2] At one stage in the eighteenth century the Holy See had approved a Mass entirely in Chinese, but for some reason the permission was not availed of.

fatal divorce between religion and what is called worldly activity in Western society. It is not necessary for us to accept the theocratic ideal of Islam and imitate them in their desire to establish the "Islamic state" wherever they are able to do it. But we must recognize that the manner in which "separation between church and state" has been realized in many Western countries has been a powerful factor in the decay of Christian faith and practice.

The Buddhists and the Hindus have an immense faith in the primacy of the soul and the possibility of demonstrating its power, and securing inner peace and harmony, by the techniques of meditation and contemplation. The practice of Yoga and Zen has certainly enabled Hindus and Buddhists to achieve very remarkable spiritual experiences. It is certain that very often these experiences, wrongly interpreted, have confirmed them in their pantheistic faith. But there is solid ground for believing that, for properly instructed Catholics, those techniques might help in the acquisition, in some degree at least, of genuine mystic union. In any case the spirit and practices of the higher aspects of these religions will help modern man to moderate his ceaseless feverish activity and turn his gaze inward. It will give even to Christians and Catholics that "interiority" in the practice of their faith which is too often lacking to them.

Finally, there is the encounter of the Church with the outermost circle which surrounds her, her dialogue with unbelievers. First, there are the Communists. Some indirect dialogue had already been exchanged with them insofar as their social challenge has been considered attentively, and has influenced the evolution of Catholic social teaching. This "indirect" dialogue is embodied in some of the pages of *Mater et magistra,* not to speak of earlier documents. But, apart from the Communists, there is the large and increasing group of "secularists" who, without being inimical to religion, are either agnostic or indifferent. If they have a religion, it is the religion of modern science, an unlimited confidence in the capacity of science to solve the problems of man's life on earth. These men are out of sympathy with many of the traditional expressions of Catholic thought, especially of Scholastic and Thomistic thought. They reject the idea of an exclusively transcendent God which they think is essential to Christianity. These men are dominant in many university circles of Western and so-called Christian countries. Their contributions to technological advance are most important and give them a commanding place in contemporary civilization. In some of the points in which they claim to differ from the Church and reject her teaching they are on common ground with many Oriental and Hindu thinkers, particularly in the attitude toward the concept of creation out of nothing by a God who stood aloof and outside creation.

In the meantime, scientists are getting alarmed at the evils arising from a technology divorced from spiritual ideals. In a recent article, Sir Julian Huxley described in the following terms the trends of modern materialistic civilization:

Motor vehicles are multiplying more than twice as fast as human beings, a trend which will eventually suffocate us by automobiliary congestion. And science and technology are multiplying more than four times as fast as man: if unchecked, well before 1999 this will submerge the intellectual world in an avalanche of scientific papers and books: no one will be able to see the wood for the multitude of trees. Science is also becoming unbalanced: a disproportionate amount of money and brain-power is devoted to physics and chemistry and technology as against biology and social sciences, to space and armaments projects as against research on contraception, ecology and exploring the "inner space" of our minds. The idea of constantly increasing economic growth is also self-defeating, and leads to cut-throat competition. In conjunction with a profit-based economic system, it tends towards overproduction of material goods and a stupid and wasteful consumerism. The frightful gap in living standards between developed and underdeveloped nations, between rich and poor countries is growing wider, while the "revolution of expectation" in the poor countries is gathering force. The continuation of this situation is bound to lead to increased misery and violence. Another alarming trend is that towards monotony, uniformity and conformism. Mass-produced goods are flooding the world; freedom of thought is stifling under conformist pressures, and life's monotony is provoking violent reactions. Meanwhile, traditional moral standards and theologies are crumbling. More and more human beings are losing their sense of significance, in what they increasingly feel is a meaningless universe.[3]

I believe that the answers to the difficulties of the scientists can be found in substance in some of the fundamental theses of Thomism as explained and commented on by the best of the modern neo-Scholastics. But we have to face the problem of using a language they will understand, and of assimilating some of the demonstrated conclusions of science and modern psychology. This explains the great vogue of the writings of Father Teilhard de Chardin among intellectuals of this type. I think that some of the best minds in the Church are inclined to work along the lines outlined by Teilhard, correcting and perfecting what has been said tentatively by him. In any case, his sense of the unity of all creation, and of the presence of spirit behind the emergence of matter and life, is in harmony with the traditional doctrine of the participated nature of finite

[3] "The Integration of Human Destiny" in *Civiltà delle Macchine*, Sept.–Oct. 1965, pp. 17–18.

being, and the need for God's sustaining presence behind it to keep it in existence. This is the point where the world of science and the world of prayer join hands in mute adoration of the God hidden behind the veil of nature—of a nature destined also from the beginning to be transfigured in Christ.

It is obvious that the world is moving towards unity both in the ideological sphere and at the social and political levels. The ideal of the dignity of the human person, of the democratic basis of government, the equality of the sexes, the opposition to racialism, are, broadly speaking, common to the whole world. So are the ideals of scientific and historical research, and the inventions of modern technology. The United Nations and its affiliated agencies have brought the nations together and are helping all of them to understand and accept these basic ideals. The Universal Declaration of Human Rights is a charter which all members have accepted. It is surprising how many of the newly independent countries have embodied them in their constitutions. The example of India is interesting, though the constitution-makers of that country did not depend mainly on the UN declaration. They were well acquainted with the humanistic traditions and political institutions of the West, and deliberately based the Indian Constitution on the English and American models. The chapters on "Fundamental Rights" and on "Directive Principles of Policy" in the Indian Constitution are perhaps the most striking example of the acceptance by the non-Christian world of political and social ideals which had evolved in the light of Christian principles.

In the context of modern nationalism it may seem unrealistic to speak of world government. Certainly "world government" involving the suppression of the cultural and social traditions which go to form the national consciousness of the people of each country is not to be thought of. But world government, in the sense of some kind of world federation, the planning of policies in the light of the common good, is not only possible but is becoming indispensable if mankind is not to destroy itself by national rivalries leading to nuclear warfare. Jawaharlal Nehru, brave leader of a people to whose independence he had consecrated the best years of his life, said that international harmony—disarmament and peace, social justice and the development of the underdeveloped nations—depended on the surrender by national states of a part of their sovereignty to an international organization. The popes have approved these ideals in unequivocal terms.

But the opposition to such world unity is very strong. It springs from the yet untamed fires of an exaggerated nationalism and that passion for national aggrandizement which pushed the world over into the vortex of two world wars. It comes also from the still powerful remnants of racialism and "caste-ism," and, in many newly independent countries, from the "revivalism" of religious and social ideas whose day has ended. These are the extreme adversaries of the desired world order on one side. Equally extreme on the other side are the followers of a secularist humanism, the fanatical "internationalists" who would suppress all idea of patriotism and devotion to one's motherland; who would reduce all mankind to a regimented and mechanized type in order to "increase production and raise standards of life."

I believe that the Catholic Church more than any other agency in the world has the true secret of reconciling the extremes and creating a true synthesis, of making them both one. She understands the human heart, the love of each man for the soil where he was born and to which are linked the tenderest memories of his childhood and the love of his dear ones. In this the Church is a mother. She is teacher also. She understands better than any one else in the world the exigencies of universal human brotherhood, and all the tragic waste involved in fratricidal war. In her doctrine and her government, throughout her long history, she has known how to adjust local traditions and national cultures with her universal message. It is indeed doubtful if outside the Church any other body can guarantee as she can the equilibrium between the old and the new, the particular and the universal.

I do not mean by this that the ideal of a world unity will not be realized unless mankind submits to the Church. Though the Church will continue to make progress in all parts of the world, and the message of the Gospel will certainly be preached to all men, we know that when the Lord comes again he will find many men without faith. There is "a mystery of evil" in the world, a power of evil of such obstinacy, of such irreconcilable hatred of good, that only the parable of Our Lord about the enemy sowing cockles among the wheat can explain it. That cockle will be allowed to grow till harvest time. So, along with, and over against the city of God, the city of pride and of self-love will exist and anti-Christ will rule in his domain.

I believe also that the spirit and achievements of the Church will be a guide and example to even those who are not of her household. Keeping firm grasp on the truths necessary for man to achieve his spiritual destiny, she will give measure and proportion to the elements needed to preserve national diversities. She believes in preserving these diversities because she wants unity in peace and freedom. Her light will shine beyond the confines of the children of light and will be reflected in many who will be wandering, perplexed and uncertain, between the two "cities."

But to shed this light, and to give this example, the Church has the need now, more than ever before in her history, of the service of the laity, of men in the world who know and love her and who wish to make her known and loved. They should help to reveal her true visage to the masses of mankind, particularly in countries where they are in a minority. It is they who must help her to overcome the exaggerations of nationalism and the dangers of secularist laicism. In the past the tendency of Catholics has been to forget the limits of genuine patriotism, and to accept in every detail "the way of life" which all nationalisms try to develop and uphold as if they had universal validity. But often there are elements in them which are not consistent with the spirit of Catholicism. The history of modern Europe, and even the present "crisis" in the Church, supply many examples of such national "deviations."

The role of the Catholic or Christian minorities in the vast non-Christian countries is even more important. The people of those countries want to profit by modern progress and at the same time they want to retain the finest elements of their ancient cultures. The Christian minority is in the strongest position to show that this is possible and that neither revolution nor reaction is the best way before them. In these countries the Church will be truly the "creator of new civilizations" insofar as she will make the adaptations needed on her part, and will call on her children to make those needed on theirs, so that a true synthesis may result. Ultimately, it is on the model of such a synthesis that the national reconstruction of those countries will be based.

But whatever the adjustments and adaptations that the Church will continually make in her onward march, the essence of her doctrinal and moral teaching will remain unchanged. It is a teaching that flows from, and is dictated by, the need to maintain an equilibrium between concepts and ideals that seem to be in contradiction because they are rooted in the fundamental antinomy which is at the heart of all created but autonomous being—equilibrium between spirit and matter, between the temporal and the eternal, between body and soul, reason and faith, authority and freedom. It is the tension arising from this inner "opposition" that gives ground to the perplexities of her action on earth. It enables us to understand how, in trying to hold these forces in balance, she may be occasionally making human mistakes, and may experience uncertainties as she keeps feeling her way. But it also gives a tragic beauty and grandeur to her enduring struggle to "keep her faith," her indefectible fidelity to her ideals. She knows that on earth she has "no lasting city"; her eyes are turned to the consummation of all things, and to the author of that consummation, Christ. In all her dialogues with the world she will keep her eyes fixed on this vision of the kingdom of God. She knows that it will avail her nothing if she gains the whole world and suffers the loss of her soul.

But we, her children, know that she will not, she cannot, lose her soul, because the "soul" of the Church is the Holy Spirit, the spirit of Jesus. His heart is the glowing centre, inspiring and sustaining her in all she does and all she endures. Through that heart she makes expiation for the sins of her children; through that heart she offers to God the uninterrupted sacrifice of their adoration, praise, and supplications, of their lives and sufferings. Holy Church, bride of Christ, mother and teacher of men, we thank you, and we bless you.

APPENDIX

There are two points, both of a rather complicated and controversial nature, to which only brief references were made in the foregoing pages. Both of these, however, are pertinent to our topic and are excellent examples of the "development" of the Church's teaching in the course of the centuries. I refer to the attitude of the Church towards slavery and towards interest on loans.

I SLAVERY

In the ancient world, slavery was accepted as completely natural. Such acceptance was based generally on two factors: first, on the right of the victor to treat prisoners of war as his personal property, and, second, on the right of a lender to the exclusive service of his debtor until the latter's debt had been paid. There were also more practical reasons for regarding slavery as necessary to human civilization; both Plato and Aristotle, for example, approved of slavery on the grounds that the "free man" of the ideal society could not be expected to engage in menial work of agricultural labor. Although there were ways of freeing, or "manumitting," a slave—and, in fact, many were freed by generous masters—the over-all situation of slaves in pagan society was not a happy one. The masters often held the absolute power of life and death over their slaves, and the latter were regarded as chattels to be bought and sold, mated and separated, punished and rewarded at the owner's whim.

Similarly, the Hebrews of the Old Testament were slave-owners, and they regarded slavery as a just and time-honoured institution. The Jewish law, however, extended its protection to the slaves of the Jews and rendered their lot more tolerable than that of slaves among the pagans.

The Christians of the first generation, whose preoccupations were exclusively spiritual and who awaited an early coming of the Kingdom, had no thought of undertaking a social revolution such as would have been implied in the abolition of slavery. Criticisms of Christianity for failing to bring about such a revolution are based upon an ignorance of historical reality—i.e., that slavery, as an institution, was as morally inoffensive to Christians as to pagans. What Christianity did was to change the moral atmosphere of society so that the conditions of the slaves were made tolerable until, gradually, slavery itself disappeared in genuinely Christian societies.

St. Paul exhorted slaves to obey their masters, and masters to treat their slaves humanely. He brought out what we may call the "egalitarian significance" of the mystery of Jesus: "All you who have been baptized in Christ's name have put on the person of Christ; no more Jew or Gentile, no more slave or freeman, no more male or female; you are all one person in Jesus Christ" (Gal. 3:27–28). Again, "You know that each of us, slave or free, will be repaid by the Lord for every task well done. You who are masters deal with them [slaves] accordingly; there is no need to threaten them; you know well enough that you and they have a Master in heaven who makes no distinction between man and man" (Eph. 6:8–9). More specially, in that exquisite Letter to Philemon, he pleaded for a runaway slave, Onesimus, whom he had "begotten in his chains," and prayed Philemon to receive him back as a brother, both of them—master and slave—being sons in Christ of Paul, "prisoner of the Lord . . .". It is a revelation of incredible gentleness, of almost motherly tenderness, from that passionate heart and indomitable will!

In keeping with this spirit, with the progress of Christianity the condition of slaves improved rapidly in the Roman Empire. Christian owners granted freedom to their slaves in increasing numbers. Ecclesiastical manumission was added to other ways by which slaves gained their liberty. The marriage of slaves was recognized as a true sacrament and not merely a cohabitation. Freed slaves could enter Holy Orders: Pope Callistus I was one such. Among the saints and martyrs most honoured by the Church were several slaves, such as saints Felicitas and Blandina. Wealthy Christians were encouraged to buy slaves in order to free them.

With the barbarian conquest of the Empire, there was no notable worsening of the condition of the slaves in the cities. But in the country there was a development which has been the occasion of sharp criticism of the Church. The need to cultivate ever-increasing areas, and the growth of feudalism, led to what appears to be slavery on a massive scale. There was an enormous number of men who were bound for life to the service of the land, without liberty to leave it and liable to be transferred to other owners when the demesne changed hands. This "villeinage," or serfdom, has been ordinarily considered slavery. While it is certain that the villeins were deprived of most of their civic rights, their fundamental religious and personal liberty was not suppressed. Only their manual services were inalienably engaged without their consent, and without right of evasion.

This condition gradually improved with the decay of feudalism, and more and more of these villeinage lands were changed into freely held acreage. (Lefebvre de Noëttes has shown, in a brilliant monograph, that forced labour began to be less necessary and serfdom diminished rapidly when, after centuries of the clumsy harnessing which obstructed their movements, horses and dray animals were yoked in a more rational manner and thus enabled to render more than double their former labour.)

Catholic moralists did not condemn outright such servitude, and this has brought on them a good deal of odium. Without trying to justify them, let us remember that among them were such men as St. Thomas Aquinas, who could not be accused of deficiency either of charity or of intelligence. So we must try to understand the position they took. They believed that, once certain fundamental human rights were assured to a man— freedom of conscience, moral liberty, integrity of family life— it was not against the natural law to bind him to lifelong physical service and total material dependence on a master. They did not say that this was a desirable state, but held it to be permissible under certain conditions. That St. Paul had accepted the fact of such a servitude, and that the master, Aristotle, had approved of it, weighed heavily with them.

Moreover, we must remember that they were speaking against a background of social conditions utterly different from our own. When democratic institutions give to every individual a political importance and the right to take part in deciding national policies, and when there is great diversity of opinions on religious and social matters, then total material dependence on another would almost certainly lead to the exerting of unfair pressure on individual liberty and to serious limitation of fundamental rights. Economically, also, we are under a regime of pitiless competition when every man has to fight his battle alone. In the ages when Christendom was a reality, when the entire European social system was organized within the structure of the Church, the monarchy, and the nobility, things were quite different. Master and serf shared a common religion which fostered a relationship of mutual respect and brotherliness, as today among the Muslims and their slaves. The spirit of paternalism ensured, even for the slave or the serf, an attitude of benevolence on the part of the lord, a sense that all of them belonged to the same family. It secured, for one's dependents, protection and food in time of war and famine. Serfs, therefore, did not ordinarily rebel against the system, and it did not appear to Catholic moralists that such "slavery" was contrary to human dignity or opposed to the natural law.

I may be permitted here a comparison with India, drawn from facts within the experience of my own lifetime. I spent my boyhood in a society where caste and "untouchability" were still in full vigour. The political and social awakening of India had begun, but had not yet penetrated into the villages. As the child of a middle-class landowning family, I saw the "untouchable" or pariah labourers of our fields living in great poverty, in poor huts which we never entered—not from indifference but from the instinctive feeling of caste prohibition. They were totally dependent on my family and had literally nothing which they could call their own. Yet, my readers must believe me when I say that there was between us a quite unusual mutual attachment and personal affection, a sense that they somehow belonged to the same great "family." There was gaiety and happiness among them, and often an independence of bearing which compelled respect.

They were in a loose way aggregated to the Hindu system and accepted its beliefs. We gave them gifts and shared their joy when there were marriages and religious festivals among them. We made no effort to apply religious pressure to them, even though we were not without zeal, and we had to content ourselves with baptizing, with due discretion, their dying infants. Their condition was worse than that of medieval serfs. Yet, it did not then occur to us that there was anything fundamentally wrong in this. Today, with freedom in India, with special privileges for the "untouchables," with chances of social and economic betterment for many of them, such a situation seems intolerable.

However, we must confess that this approval of even a modified kind of slavery, though in itself intelligible, had, at a later stage, unhappy consequences on the minds of Catholics. When the Muslims established themselves in Europe with their brilliant civilization and the practice of slavery in the full sense, Europeans lost something of the Christian attitude to human liberty and dignity which had developed during earlier centuries. Then followed the long period of religious and moral decadence which preceded the Great Schism and the Protestant Reformation. Just at that time, Europe discovered America and the Portuguese conquered Angola. In Africa, Christians saw slavery flourishing without opposition. They soon thought of slavery among non-Europeans, and particularly among Africans and American Indians, as normal. Before long, they traded on that fact and began that rapacious commerce of slaves, African and Indian, with all its attendant cruelties, which is one of the greatest blots on European civilization and on the record of so-called Christian people.

In this resurgence of slavery in its most revolting forms among Christian people, the role of the Church is the least humiliating. We have spoken of the religious orders founded to redeem Christian slaves from Muslim masters. The popes, from Pius II to Pius X, denounced cruelty towards Negroes and Indians. We have noted the role of Bartolomeo Las Casas in the defence of the Indians, the efforts of the Jesuits to protect them from slave raids in the Reductions of Paraguay, the heroic work of St. Peter Claver among the Negro slaves at Cartagena. Modern missionary action among slaves in Africa is in keeping with these examples.

It is true that the nineteenth-century movement for the emancipation of slaves started in the Protestant and Anglo-Saxon countries, and that some of the Catholic countries of

South America were the last to free their slaves. But we should not forget that the Protestant and Anglo-Saxon countries had been the most pitiless in the slave trade and in the ill treatment of Indians; and that, till almost yesterday, the British practised a system of "indentured labour" in their colonies of South Africa, the Fiji Islands, and the Caribbean islands, a system hardly different from medieval slavery. I shall not speak of the near-slavery of the industrial proletariat in the palmy days of European "liberalism" and capitalism. It remains true that the Catholic Church, while abstaining, consistently with her spirit, from stirring the victims of tyranny—political, economic, and social—to rebellion and revolution, has ever exerted her influence to humanize their condition and ensure for them a minimum of personal dignity and freedom.

II INTEREST ON LOANS

Here, again, the teaching of the Church presents problems of unusual complexity and illustrates an evolution which, unlike her teaching concerning slavery, is far from having reached its term. It affects questions which have a connection with actual economic problems. All great religions have, from their earliest times, condemned the levying of interest on the loan of articles considered consumable, particularly when given in order to help someone in need. Money was deemed unproductive, not consumable, and thus the principles of justice and of brotherly charity forbade the collecting of interest. The exhortations in the Psalms against lending on interest will be easily recalled. The Old Testament ideal of justice and goodness included prominently the readiness to lend to the needy without hope of material reward. Catholic condemnation of interest as being usury is found in the writings of the fathers—St. Clement of Alexandria, St. John Chrysostom, St. Ambrose, St. Jerome. St. Thomas treats the subject at length in the *Summa* (IIa–IIae

Q.78, art. 1–4). Benedict XIV resumed the traditional teaching in the encyclical *Vix pervenit* (1735).

These principles retained their vigour in a pastoral and agricultural milieu. But they began to be questioned when the growth of trade and commerce, and the increasing circulation of metallic currency, changed the state of things. Money became an essential element in productive enterprises. Moreover, there was always risk of loss, or of devaluation, between the time of lending and the time of repayment. Gradually, the moralists who had condemned interest unconditionally were led to consider it a passive, but effective, partnership in a productive undertaking. Hence, the payment of interest did not seem contrary to commutative justice. There was, moreover, no question of aiding the needy in such commercial undertakings. Calvin seems to have been the first well-known religious leader to defend lending money on interest. Catholic moralists in increasing numbers followed. In the seventeenth century, the Jesuit theologians of Austria were the first to approve openly, in favour of the great Catholic banking family of the Fuggers, the levying of a 5 per cent interest.[1]

Even while this was being increasingly accepted, the moralists never failed to insist that the conciliar and papal condemnations of usury still were in force. The problem was to decide what should be considered a *reasonable* rate of interest. This should obviously be fixed by an examination of conditions in a given time and place, and, after the example of the French revolutionary government, all civil governments approved the levying of interest and took steps to fix, as far as possible, a legal and reasonable rate. Canon 1543 of the *Code of Canon Law* sanctions a reasonable rate of interest, and in certain conditions even one higher than the legal rate. We can easily im-

[1] See Fr. J. Brodrick's fascinating book, *The Economic Doctrine of the Jesuits.*

agine conditions where the purchasing power of money owing to inflation is not reflected in the "legal rate," and so a higher one becomes permissible.

Nevertheless, the alarming fact remains that, in a modern economic system, both in the industrial and financial sphere, it is possible and it is considered allowable, to make profits which amount to highly usurious rates of interest and render altogether unjust returns for capital expended. Therefore, such profits are in themselves morally reprehensible. This is even more true of stock exchange speculations. Such enormous gains lead to inflation and the devaluation of the savings of honest people, who are thus deprived of the fruits of their labour. These and allied abuses have been repeatedly described and denounced in the social encyclicals. A Christian social order must find means of eliminating them. Hence, the teaching of the Church on interest, and on the allied subjects of fair profits and just wages, is of burning actuality.

BIBLIOGRAPHY

BREMOND, HENRI. *Histoire Littéraire du Sentiment Religieux en France;* Volume I, *L'Humanisme Chrétien.* Paris, Librairie Bloud et Gay, 1923.

BRODRICK, JAMES. *Saint Francis Xavier.* Garden City, Doubleday & Company, Inc. (Image Books), 1957.

CHESTERTON, G. K. *St. Francis of Assisi.* Garden City, Doubleday & Company, Inc. (Image Books), 1957.

CONSTANTINI, CELSO CARDINAL. *La Réforme des Missions au XX Siècle.* Paris, Maison Casterman, 1958.

CRONIN, VINCENT. *A Pearl to India.* New York, E. P. Dutton & Co., Inc., 1959.

———. *The Wise Man from the West.* New York, E. P. Dutton & Co., Inc., 1955.

CUTTAT, JEAN ALBERT. *La Rencontre des Religions.* Paris, Aubier, 1961.

DAHMEN, PIERRE. *Un Jésuite Brahme, Robert de Nobili.* Louvain, Musaeum Lessianum, 1924.

DANIEL-ROPS, HENRI. *History of the Church of Christ;* particularly Volume I, *The Church of Apostles and Martyrs* (1962), Volume IV, *The Protestant Reformation* (1963), and Volume V, *The Catholic Reformation* (1964). Garden City, Doubleday & Company, Inc. (Image Books).

DAWSON, CHRISTOPHER. *Religion and Culture.* New York, Sheed and Ward, Inc., 1948.

FARQUHAR, J. N. *Modern Religious Movements in India.* New York, The Macmillan Company, 1929.

GIRAULT, RENÉ. *Dialogues aux Frontières de l'Église.* Paris, Éditions Ouvrières, 1965.

GRANDMAISON, LEONCE DE, *Jesus Christ.* Paris, Beauchesne et Fils, 1926.

HERBERT, JEAN. *Spiritualité Hindoue.* Paris, Éditions Albin Michel, 1947.

HUGHES, PHILIP. *A Popular History of the Catholic Church.* Garden City, Doubleday & Company, Inc. (Image Books), 1954.

JUDD, PETER (ed.). *African Independence.* New York, Dell Publishing Company, 1962.

LACOMBE, OLIVIER. *Chemins de l'Inde.* Paris, Éditions Alsatia, 1956.

LANTERNARI, VITTORIO. *Movimenti Religiosi di Libertà e di Salvezza dei Popoli Oppressi.* Milan, Editore Feltrinelli, 1960.

MACAULAY, THOMAS B. *Essays.* New York, E. P. Dutton & Co., Inc., 1960.

MC NEILL, WILLIAM. *The Rise of the West.* Chicago, Chicago University Press, 1962.

MÂLE, ÉMILE. *L'Art Religieux après le Concile de Trente.* Paris, Librairie Armand Colin, 1932.

MARGOLIOUTH, DAVID S. *Mohammedanism.* London, Butterworth & Co., Ltd., 1928.

NEWMAN, JOHN HENRY CARDINAL. *Apologia Pro Vita Sua.* Garden City, Doubleday & Company, Inc. (Image Books), 1956.
———. *An Essay on the Development of Christian Doctrine.* Garden City, Doubleday & Company, Inc. (Image Books), 1960.

PANIKKAR, K. M. *Asia and Western Dominance.* London, George Allen, 1953.

RAGHAVAN, V. *The Indian Heritage* (Anthology of Texts).
Bangalore, Indian Institute of Culture, 1956.

RIZZA, ARMANDO. *Buddhismo in Risveglio.* Milan, Pontificio Isti-
tuto delle Missioni Estere, 1964.

ROSA, GIUSEPPE DE, "Volto Segreto della Chiesa," *La Civiltà
Cattolica.* Rome, 1964.

SMITH, CANTWELL. *Islam in Modern History.* Princeton,
Princeton University Press, 1959.

STORRY, RICHARD. *A History of Modern Japan.* London, Penguin
Books, Ltd., 1960.

TEILHARD DE CHARDIN, PIERRE. *The Divine Milieu.* New York,
Harper & Row, Publishers, Inc., 1960.

———. *The Phenomenon of Man.* New York, Harper & Row,
Publishers, Inc., 1965.

TEMPELS, PLACIDE. *Bantu Philosophy.* Manuscript translation by
Rev. Colin King of the Maryknoll Mission.

TOYNBEE, ARNOLD. *A Journey round the World.* New York, Oxford University Press, 1965.

———. *The World and the West.* New York, Oxford University
Press, 1957.

WALLACE, W. *From Evangelical to Catholic by Way of the East.*
Ranchi, Catholic Press, 1920.

ZAEHNER, R. C. *At Sundry Times.* New York, Humanities
Press, 1958.

———. *Matter and Spirit.* New York, Harper & Row, Publishers, Inc., 1963.

———. *Mysticism, Sacred and Profane.* New York, Oxford University Press, 1957.